BLACK GOD

AN INTRODUCTION TO THE WORLD'S RELIGIONS AND THEIR BLACK GODS

DR. SUPREME UNDERSTANDING

PART OF THE SCIENCE OF SELF SERIES

Published by Supreme Design Publishing. PO Box 10887, Atlanta, GA 30310. Visit us online at www.supremedesignpublishing.com

Although the author and publisher have made every effort to ensure the accuracy and completeness of information contained in this book, we assume no responsibility for errors, inaccuracies, omissions, or any inconsistency herein. Any perceived slights of people, places, or organizations are not intended to be malicious in nature.

Supreme Design Publishing is a registered business member of the 360 Movement. Find out more about our principles, our programs, and our network at www.the360movement.com

Supreme Design Publishing is also a member of the Tree Neutral™ initiative, which works to offset paper consumption through tree planting. Our books are printed on long-lasting acid-free paper. When it is available, we choose paper that has been manufactured by environmentally responsible practices. These may include using trees grown in sustainable forests, incorporating recycled paper, minimizing chlorine in bleaching, or recycling the energy produced at the paper mill.

TreeNeutral

ISBN: 978-1-935721-04-8

Library of Congress Control Number: 2013922346

Wholesale Discounts. Special discounts (up to 55% off of retail) are available on quantity purchases. For details, visit our website, contact us by mail at the address above, Attention: Wholesale Orders, or email us at orders@supremedesignonline.com

Individual Sales. Supreme Design publications are available for retail purchase, or can be requested, at most bookstores. They can also be ordered directly from the Supreme Design Publishing website, at www.SupremeDesignPublishing.com

FIND MORE BOOKS LIKE THIS AT
WWW.THESCIENCEOFSELF.COM

FOREWORD

BY BISHOP HENRY MCNEAL TURNER

"I worship a Negro God. I believe God is a Negro.
Negroes should worship a God who is a Negro."
— Bishop Henry McNeal Turner, 1898

For a lot of us, the idea of a Black God is difficult to process. If you're reading this book, and haven't yet doused it in holy water and thrown it into a fire, you're probably at least somewhat open to the idea. But there's a good chance that most of your friends and family aren't. Of course, things are changing. More and more people are considering new ideas, so the idea of God being Black isn't as hard for people to process as it was before. But this isn't a new idea. In fact, for as long as Black people have been talking about God, people have been debating this idea.

In the following section, you'll read the response that AME Bishop Henry McNeal Turner gave in 1898, when a newspaper editorial called him demented for saying that God is a Negro.

"GOD IS A NEGRO"
BY BISHOP HENRY MCNEAL TURNER

We have as much right biblically and otherwise to believe that God is a Negro, as you buckra, or white, people have to believe that God is a fine looking, symmetrical and ornamented white man. For the bulk of you, and all the fool Negroes of the country, believe that God is white-skinned, blue-eyed, straight-haired, projecting-nosed, compressed-lipped, and finely-robed white gentleman sitting upon a throne somewhere in the heavens.

Every race of people since time began who have attempted to describe their God by words, or by paintings, or by carvings, or by any other form or figure have conveyed the idea that the God who made them and shaped their destinies was symbolized in themselves, and why should not the Negro believe that he resembles God as much as other people? We do not believe that there is any hope for a race of people who do not believe that they look like God.

Demented though we be, whenever we reach the conclusion that God or even that Jesus Christ, while in the flesh, was a white man, we shall hang our gospel trumpet upon the willow and cease to preach.

We had rather be an atheist and believe in no God or a pantheist and believe that all nature is God, than to believe in the personality of a God and not believe that He is Negro. Blackness is much older than whiteness, for black was here before white, if the Hebrew word, *coshach,* or *chasack*, has any meaning.

We do not believe in the eternity of matter, but we do believe that chaos floated in infinite darkness or blackness, millions, billions, quintillions and eons of years before God said, "Let there be light," and that during that time God had no material light Himself and was shrouded in darkness, so far as human comprehension is able to grasp the situation.

Yet we are no stickler as to God's color, anyway, but if He has any we should prefer to believe that it is nearer symbolized in the blue sky above us and the blue water of the seas and oceans; but we certainly protest against God being a white man or against God being white at all; abstract as this theme must forever remain while we are in the flesh.

This is one of the reasons we favor African emigration, or Negro nationalization, wherever we can find a domain, for as long as we remain among whites, the Negro will believe that the devil is black and that he (the Negro) favors the devil, and that God is white and the (the Negro) bears no resemblance to Him, and the effect of such a sentiment is contemptuous and degrading, and one-half of the Negro race will be trying to get white and the other half will spend their days trying to be white men's scullions in order to please the whites; and the time they should be giving to the study of such things will dignify and make our race great will be devoted to studying about how unfortunate they are in not being white.

We conclude these remarks by repeating for the information of the Observer what it adjudged us demented for – God is a Negro.

TABLE OF CONTENTS

INTRODUCTION

WHAT TO EXPECT

"The earliest gods and messiahs on all the continents were black. Research has yielded an impressive amount of material on the subject." – Historian J.A. Rogers

Have you ever heard that Christ was Black? What about the Buddha? They weren't alone. Many of the world's first deities and divinities, both male and female, were originally depicted as Black. That means dark skin, woolly hair, broad nose, and the kind of personality that made the world pay attention. In this book, historian Supreme Understanding explores the many Black gods of the ancient world, from Africa to the Near East, to Europe, to India, to China, to Japan, to Australia, all the way to the Black Gods of the Americas.

Who were they? How did they come to be worshipped? And what does this mean for us today? These are the questions we'll answer in this work.

THE BACKGROUND TO THIS BOOK

Throughout this book, you'll find dozens of quotes from books that are quite old. In many cases, we're talking about more than a century old. In some cases, even older. Naturally, some of the language will be difficult and dry. Some of it might even sound racist.

So why am I quoting all these old books? Because that's when they were still telling the truth! Why? Because they believed we'd never read these books! In these old books (often the ones that didn't circulate much) you'll find white historians, theologians, anthropologists, and ethnographers making incredible admissions about race and religion, the likes of which you're very unlikely to find in a mainstream publication today.

In most cases, the facts remain the same as they were stated back then (for example, the Mayan Ekchuah is still most definitely painted with black skin), but scholars have come up with new ways to dance around these facts (e.g. "Ekchuah's color is symbolic of chocolate"). Older texts will often (not always) present the facts much more directly. And there's no better example than the epic work of British historian Godfrey Higgins.

ANACALYPSIS: THE UNVEILING

Over 200 years ago, Higgins began his research into the origins of the world's religions. He researched for nearly twenty years, devoting almost ten hours a day to this pursuit. He later admitted:

> In the first ten years of my search I may fairly say, I found nothing which I sought for. In the latter part of the twenty, the quantity of matter has so crowded in upon me, that I scarcely know how to dispose of it.

Higgins did not live to see the publication of his work. His son published his research posthumously in 1833. The book, titled *Anacalypsis: An Inquiry into the Origin of Languages, Nations and Religions*, came out in two volumes, together spanning over 1,400 pages. What was said in this book was monumental.

Higgins prefaced his work with an open acknowledgement that few would fully understand what he'd attempted to present, noting:

> I think it right to warn my reader, that there are more passages than one in the book, which are of that nature, which will be perfectly understood by my Masonic friends, but which my engagements prevent me explaining to the world at large.

But Higgins had no interest in the occult or the esoteric. What was it that he could not explain? Could any of it have made its way from his notes into the published book? Perhaps.

Higgins attested to the deep symbolism behind our letters and numbers, the origins of the world's secret societies, and many other issues you won't find discussed in other books of his time. But one of his most controversial findings can be summed up in the following quote from *Anacalypsis*:

> We have found the Black complexion or something relating to it whenever we have approached the origin of nations...In short all the...deities were black. They remained as they were first...in very ancient times.[1]

In other words, most of the gods of the ancient world were originally depicted with black skin. Not because of an artistic convention or some symbolic significance, but for a much more literal reason. Higgins wastes no words in connecting these legends with actual Black men and women who once walked the earth and inspired legions of followers.

WAS HIGGINS INSANE?

Was Higgins a "fringe" lunatic or weirdo who no one respected? Nothing suggests it. In fact he was a decorated archaeologist and Fellow of the Society of Antiquaries. As a county magistrate, he demanded better treatment for the mentally ill, criticized excessive taxation of the working class, campaigned for Parliamentary Reform, and fought against the exploitation of children in factories. In his death, he was remembered by his parish as a "political radical, reforming county magistrate and idiosyncratic historian of religions." Not a lunatic.

Well then, where did these claims come from? Was he an Afrocentrist with an agenda? Unlikely, considering that, well, Godfrey Higgins was white. And this was nearly 200 years ago. Higgins had no reason to lie. In fact, his claims about the Blackness of the world's first deities didn't win him any new fans. His books were only printed in limited editions, perhaps primarily intended for a Masonic audience...not the public at large.

Fortunately, his work has survived into the present day. And we now have a wealth of resources which we can use to research Higgins' claims. In this book, we'll discuss the gods of the ancient world – many of whom are still worshiped today – and explore the idea that these deities were once widely known to be Black. We'll also explore how these figures came to be worshiped, and what happened to these Black deities...many of whom are now thought of as colorless or white.

This book introduces the Black gods of Asia, Africa, the Americas, Europe, and dozens of other places throughout the world. In the follow-up to this book, we'll talk about the history of religion itself, tracing the roots of worship and organized religion back to the same place these Black gods originally came from.

HOW THIS BOOK IS DIFFERENT

Reputable Sources: This book is meant to be a reference book, almost like an encyclopedia of Black gods. The sources are well-documented, and I almost never use sources that weren't taken seriously when they were published. I often use lengthy block quotes just to "prove" that I'm not employing a creative license in reinterpreting what was said in the original sources.

No flim-flam: As I noted in *The Science of Self, Volume One*, there are far too many authors and "experts" who either don't understand research methodology, or would simply rather not use it. So we've got a ton of misinformation flooding bookstores, websites, and YouTube, masquerading as sound research. Sometimes, you can't even find the quotes being quoted in the original sources. I'm not a fan of that kind of "scholarship." I think it makes us look like idiots and frauds.

Easy Reading: At the same time, I'm comfortable enough with the quality of my research to write in a tone that feels comfortable to me and my audience. Sometimes, this tone sounds academic, and other times, it sounds very conversational.

Still Scholarly: If I knew that everyone would take these statements seriously no matter how it was written, I'd write everything in the same colloquial tone I used in *How to Hustle and Win*. But because I know there are many of you who'll want to quote this book in your research papers and presentations, I'll write in a way that makes it easier to convince your professors and colleagues that we're not just a bunch of hood dudes taking wild guesses.

If the long quotes and academic-sounding language make you uncomfortable, drink some strong coffee or somethin. And keep reading. Before long, I'll say something regular again.

HOW TO READ THIS BOOK

The following guidelines should make it easier to read and understand this book:

❏ Think of this book like a reference book. Unlike *The Science of Self, Volume One*, you don't necessarily have to read this book from front to back. You can skip around, because this work is meant to be encyclopedic like *The Hood Health Handbook* – a useful reference on over dozens of deities, traditions, and other topics.

❏ If you come across a difficult concept, a technical-sounding quote, or a section that simply doesn't catch your interest, skip it. Often, those long block quotes are followed by an explanation in laymen's terms. And what doesn't catch you on your first read might catch your interest on your second read.

❏ If you don't feel like keeping a dictionary next to you while you read, there are free dictionary apps for most smartphones, and Dictionary.com is easy to use as well. Wherever we can, we define tough words, but you still might run into a few that you need to clarify.

☐ When you read, write in the margins and highlight text as often as you can. You may even want to use one of those colorful sticky-tab bookmarking systems.

☐ It's also helpful to keep a notebook where you take notes and record your thoughts.

☐ We always ask that you share our work with others. We appreciate when you take pictures of our books and share them online, or post quotes (with the necessary credits!). SDP thrives off word-of-mouth.

☐ At the same time, you may not get great results if you introduce this book to a friend who doesn't like reading. You may need to start with a book like *How to Hustle and Win,* or *Rap, Race, and Revolution*, or *Knowledge of Self*. Those books are better suited for general audiences. This book, like *The Science of Self, Volume One*, is much heavier reading and will be tough for the uninitiated.

IF JESUS' COLOR DIDN'T MATTER

Depiction of Christ
Rome, 530 AD

YOU WOULDN'T CARE IF I SAID HE WAS BLACK.

BUT THE WAY IT BOTHERS YOU TO HEAR THAT SAYS A LOT.

www.knowledgeofself.us

☐ Still, carry the book with you. We delay our eBook releases (sometimes for a year or more) for a reason! We want people to bring this knowledge into the REAL world. We love the internet as much as you do, but we're trying to kill all that disconnectedness and "reinvent the world" by bringing our people back together. (You'll get it when you read this book). So take this book out with you, and let those random conversations begin. You'll be surprised how much good can come from something that seems so insignificant.

☐ Just don't bombard folks with too much "truth" at once. Let them ask the questions. And start conversations, not "conversions." We're not going to succeed by tearing each other down. We all have something we care about, so "respect" and "understanding" are critical when we share information like this.

GOD AND RACE

DOES RACE MATTER?

"As so much else that is mistakenly thought of as "new," the concept of a Black God or Black Christ is quite ancient." – Herbert Aptheker, A Documentary History of the Negro People in the United States

Before you tell yourself that God is "above color" and dismiss this work as frivolous, I want you to read the following pages. In this chapter, we'll explore why the topic of a Black God is not simply important, but critical to our understanding of theology, history, and the world as it is today. Understanding why so many of the world's first deities were Black is not simply about having a better understanding of the world's religions, but it can help us better understand everything – especially ourselves.

You may have heard of the 1947 doll study, conducted by legendary sociologists Kenneth and Mamie Clark. In this study, Black children were given a choice between a Black doll and a white doll, who were the same in every way except color. Given this choice, most Black children chose the white doll, and said they believed the white doll was nicer.[2] It was such a revealing study that it played a significant role in the 1954 Brown v. Board of Education case. But here's what you may not know. This tragic study was actually reproduced only a few years ago. And guess what? The results were the same.[3] Still. What does this say about us and the way we've been conditioned?

Now, for most people, God is a big deal. Your idea of God has a lot to do with your idea of you. So what happens when the way we think about the divine is not so far removed from the way the children in the doll study thought about beauty? Whether we'd like to admit it or not, many of us are subconsciously conditioned to see God in very personal terms – often as "flesh-and-blood" as anyone else we know. So it's worthwhile to examine the "color issue" when it comes to God as well. This is where we'll begin.

IS GOD A WHITE MAN?

Throughout the world, wherever we find a history of European colonization, we find that changes in power went hand in hand with changes in theology. That is – to say it in laymen's terms – wherever white folks went, they made the people believe that God was a white man. Meanwhile, their native gods – who looked like them – were reimagined as demons, devils, and "pagan deities" worshiped in secret. This happened everywhere. And "everywhere" isn't an exaggeration. I mean everywhere.

"When the missionaries came to Africa they had the Bible and we had the land. They said 'Let us pray.' We closed our eyes. When we opened them we had the Bible and they had the land." – Desmond Tutu

South African Archbishop Desmond Tutu was being quite literal when he said the words above. In the West, things were worse. There, having been stripped of their indigenous languages and traditions, enslaved Africans were more susceptible to foreign ideas. As historian J.A. Rogers notes in his classic work, *Sex and Race*, "The American and the West Indian Negro with no traditions of their own have a white God."

This "education" was intentional. If you've seen the phenomenal film *12 Years a Slave*, you saw how readings from the Bible were "cherry-picked" to support slavery and the idea of Black inferiority. Does the Bible actually teach that Blacks are inferior? Hardly. Yet religion has historically been a tool used by those in power to further support their power in the hearts and minds of those who believe.

Thus, few of us have any idea what most religious traditions – as they were taught by their earliest proponents, at least – actually have to say about God. For many of us, we are subconsciously conditioned to think of God in white terms. We are also conditioned to find it deeply offensive when it is suggested that God is Black. This is not by accident, but by design.

In *Cause and Contrast: An Essay on the American Crisis*, published in 1862, Southern Baptist T.W. MacMahon lays out his defense for the institution of slavery. MacMahon argued that Black people were not equal to whites because neither God, nor any divine being, had ever appeared to humanity in dark skin:

> For it would be a most difficult effort of the mind, even in an abandoned and confirmed white abolitionist, to imagine a sable [dark-skinned] Holy Mary or St. Cecilia…Again, if [Blacks were] equal to us in organism and intellectual endowments, it is no less singular than remarkable, that God should have withheld the

prophets of His Word from being of their race; since no negro Saviour of Mankind – no Socrates, Isaiah, Brahma, or Mohammed, has yet condescended to enlighten the world with any civilized system of Theogony.[4]

In other words, so long as it could be upheld that God, his angels, his son, and his saints were all white, and only the Devil was black, Blacks would "know their place" at the bottom of the society.

Imagine what would happen, these theologians whispered in private, should they come to learn otherwise?

DOES GOD HAVE NO COLOR?

Bishop Henry McNeal Turner

Over a century ago, Bishop Henry McNeal Turner knew that most of his congregation had grown up being taught – either explicitly or implicitly – that God and Jesus were white. Turner said it would be better to be an atheist or pantheist than to worship a personal God who looks nothing like the persons worshipping him.

It's this sentiment that eventually gave rise to the modern cliché "My God doesn't have a color." It wasn't some scientific rationalism or Neo-Platonism. It was simply developed as a way to dance around what this God might look like. You see, people who say this aren't typically pantheists or animists. They don't think of God as some universal force, because – if they did – they might see God in themselves as well.

Rather, most still have a personal God, typically a "Father in Heaven" kinda guy. They say he doesn't have a color, but in their subconscious minds, he does. He's still white. And this is not some insignificant thing. Our concept of God is critical to our self-concept and the way we grow and develop as individuals and as a community. This is why it's important for us to undo the psychological trauma that was done via the concept of a white God.

WHITE IMAGES AND PSYCHOLOGICAL CONDITIONING

Have you ever thought about what happens when Black and brown people grow up, only having seen their sacred figures portrayed as white people? More than 100 years ago, Presbyterian minister Edward Wilmot Blyden found these issues worthy of his study. In 1875, Blyden wrote an essay titled "Mohammedanism and the Negro Race" where he argued that Islam avoided such issues. He noted that both Judaism and Islam prohibited any artwork attempting to represent the divine, while the Christian world produced mountains of iconic statues and sacred imagery.

The problem with this, Blyden explained, was that…

> [T]o the Negro all these exquisite representations exhibited only the physical characteristics of a foreign race; and while they tended to quicken the tastes and refine the sensibilities of that race, they had only a depressing influence upon the Negro, who felt that he had neither part nor lot so far as the physical character was concerned, in those splendid representations.

In other words, Black people could find themselves nowhere in any of this imagery.

Edward Wilmot Blyden

How did this affect Black Christians? Blyden, a pioneer of Black Nationalism, continued:

> The Christian Negro, abnormal in his development, pictures God and all beings remarkable for their moral and intellectual qualities with the physical characteristics of the Europeans, and deems it an honor if he can approximate – by a mixture of his blood, however irregularly achieved – in outward appearance at least to the ideal thus forced upon him by the physical accompaniments of all excellence. In this way he loses that 'sense of dignity of human nature' observable in his Mohammedan brother.

In other words, looking at all this sacred white stuff makes us ashamed to be ourselves. We subconsciously identify with white power and privilege, having never seen ourselves cast in the light of divinity, royalty, or any other great stature. The fact that "Black history" typically begins with slavery is another part of this same process of miseducation.

This is why you'll encounter people who'll say "Jesus' color doesn't matter." Well, if that was the case, it shouldn't matter if we say God and Jesus are Black. If it doesn't matter, who cares if we say that? The reason why people care is because they're still attached to white Gods and they're scared to consider anything differently.

If only they knew that all the world's traditions originally portrayed God as Black.

GOD IN THE FLESH

Don't get the premise of this book wrong. I'm not saying that all the world's cultures have described God as a flesh-and-blood Black man. Most cultures have a creation story, and these stories often recognize a time before the physical universe existed. This is where we find the God who was God before there was an Earth to inhabit.

Throughout this book, you'll see examples of this "transcendent" idea of God, who is often self-created or had no beginning. Most of the world's cultures didn't bother to describe this Creator in physical language, rather using abstract terms that refer to a consciousness that predated the physical world.

In the physical world, however, this God becomes manifest as an "immanent" being. Not simply a supreme "mind," this God is a "Supreme Being" because he exists in the world. The question is HOW does this God exist? Most of the world's cultures describe him like a man, often the father of all men, and sometimes the first man himself. Most people who are familiar with the traditions of their religion know this already. What many do not know is the skin that this God almost always chose to "veil" himself in was black.

In this book, we'll explore all the traditions where this is the case, as well as the reasons for why these people – even as far as China and Alaska – described their most powerful gods as Black men.

BLACK GODS – WHY AND HOW?

Throughout the ancient world, we find Black gods everywhere. And not just the "father of humanity" figures, but gods of all sorts. Warrior gods, healer gods, gods of prosperity, and "culture heroes" who taught people everything they knew. And they were Black.

But why? There are many reasons. For some scholars, it seems easy to dismiss these portrayals as "artistic conventions" or "symbolic" in some sense. Upon further examination, however, the reasons appear more literal and historical.

In 1900, in an early study on Krishna and other Black gods across Europe and Asia, William Crooke wrote:

Krishna

> The question of the explanation of the origin of these black gods is extremely complex.

In some cases we may suspect that they represent a racial type familiar to the people who first introduced this form of worship. We must remember that among some races, blackness of complexion is not alone considered not unbecoming, but is even admired. One of the titles of the Zulu kings, for instance, was "You who are black;" and the lady in the Canticles [Songs of Solomon] says, "I am black but comely, O daughters of Jerusalem."

We find the Egyptian queen, Nofritari [Nefertare], consort of Ahmosis, identified with Isis and depicted as a black-skinned goddess. Hence we can explain why St. Benedito, a black negro saint is worshipped on the Amazon, and on the Gold Coast [of West Africa] the white man's God is said to be black...[5]

What Crooke is suggesting here is that a careful study of religion – across the world – will reveal that the first gods and goddesses were actually based on the worship of men and women. And, more often than not, these men and women were Black.

Who were these people before they became deified? And why were these people held in such high regard? And how did they come to be worshipped?

In this book, we'll focus on dozens of Black gods across the world.

Some of them may be quite familiar to you. In fact, some people may find it difficult to deal with the fact that *their* God was originally a Black god. Some readers will find themselves with questions and doubts they never had before.

That's okay. Just keep reading, and I promise you'll be satisfied with the answers you arrive at. And relax. We'll be respectful, because these subjects deserve respect. As Greek historian Herodotus (who spoke quite often about these Black gods) once remarked:

> The whole conduct of Cambyses towards the Egyptian gods, sanctuaries and priests, convinces me that this King was in the highest degree insane; for otherwise he would not have insulted the worship and holy things of a people.

It's our hope that this information be put to good use – as in building understanding and solidarity between those of us from different traditions – not for the purpose of being rude and argumentative regarding the beliefs of others. Remember, a lot of people will have put this book down before even getting *this* far. If you want to engage others in discussions like these, you've got to be respectful.

In the follow-up to this book, we'll explore the roots of these traditions, digging into the concepts of ancestor worship, divine kingship, and how historical records became cultural mythology. In other words, we'll tell the story of how all these religions came to be. For now, I want to introduce you to the Gods.

A quick side note: Some of you might be saying to yourself, "What about the goddesses, you sexist pig?" Relax. I'm quite the opposite. In this book, we're focusing on male gods. But we'll also cover a few female deities (who are also Black). We'll talk about Kali, the Black Madonna, Auset (Isis), and a few others. But I'd prefer to dedicate an entire book to the subject of the *divine feminine*, rather than try to cram everyone in one book. After all, I know of enough Black female divinities to fill a book the same size as this one. So we'll do just that. I'm thinking of titling it *Mother Nature is a Black Woman*.

THE GODS OF ASIA

FROM INDIA TO JAPAN

"In India black gods abound. Besides those to whom statues of black stone are dedicated, of which more later on, we have Siva and Rahu, Vishnu, Tara, and Kali-devi." – W. Crooke, "Legends of the Krishna"

If you've ever been to India, then you know that you can find some of the world's darkest people there. And not just pockets of them, but millions of them. Many of them look like East Africans, while others look more like Australian Aborigines. Some even have the woolly hair texture you'd typically associate with African people.

The Black people of India are everywhere, because India was once a Black civilization. So it makes sense that most of India's gods, at least those that are indigenous to the region, are dark-skinned themselves.

These Black gods were not limited to India, but were spread throughout all of Asia. Crooke associated the complexion of these gods with the historical presence of black-skinned people.

He wasn't alone. In Buckley's *Cities of the Ancient World*, Kenneth R. Mackenzie reports:

> From the wooly texture of the hair, I am inclined to assign to the Buddha of India, the Fuhi of China, the Sommonacom of the Siamese, the Zaha of the Japanese, and the Quetzalcoatl of the Mexicans, the same, and indeed an African, or rather Nubian, origin.

Who were these Gods? Where did they come from? Why were they worshipped? In this chapter, we'll answer those questions.

THE BLACK GODS OF INDIA

AN INTRODUCTION TO HINDUISM

Hinduism is the most widespread religious tradition in India, with over 900 million adherents. Because Hindus don't typically proselytize, or attempt to convert others, Hinduism isn't as widespread in other parts of the world. So India and Hinduism kinda go hand-in-hand. In fact, India was once known to Westerners as *Hindustan*, and the words "Hindu" and "Indian" were considered synonymous.

What do Hindus believe? Many things. After all, Hinduism – like many other world religions – was born from a wide variety of indigenous traditions being blended together under a common umbrella. There's also an undeniable influence from the West. Not the West as in modern Europe or America, but the ancient west: the Caucasus. A little after 2000 BC, hordes of Indo-European-speaking people came into India. They came in small waves, but eventually toppled indigenous rule and took over. This is known to historians as the "Aryan conquest of India."

When this happened, it wasn't just a military takeover. These people also transformed the religious and political philosophy of India. This is when many of the indigenous Black gods were turned into Black demons. In their place, there were now white gods. In fact, an entire social system – known as the *varna* (or "color") system – was introduced so that dark-skinned people could occupy India's lowest social castes, while the Aryans and their descendants were – by God's law – now at the top of the social order. Those who did not "mix" into this new system became "untouchables."

But think about it. There's no way you can simply take over someone's land and kick out all of their old gods. Cortez tried this with the Aztecs in 1519 and they nearly killed him and his entire army. Instead, those who hope to take over successfully, and with least amount of rebellion possible, will instead "keep" some of the old gods. They'll turn some of them into "bad" gods or villains, while raising up others – so long as they can control how that god is described. This is what the Aryans did with Krishna, one of the most prominent gods of Hinduism.

KRISHNA, INCARNATION OF THE SUPREME GOD

Krishna is one of the most important gods in the Hindu pantheon. He is the central figure in the *Mahabharata*, one of the most important Hindu epics, and is regarded as an incarnation of the Supreme God Vishnu by millions of Hindus everywhere.

Krishna is almost always depicted with black skin. When he is not, he is depicted with blue skin, but it remains understood that this is only symbolic of his true black color.

BUT WHY IS HE BLACK?

If you Google "Why is Krishna Black?" you might come across the following explanation, which is based entirely on Hindu scripture:

Once Mother Yashoda called Krishna and asked Him: Darling Krishna, people doubt who you belong to?

Krishna: To you of course mother.

Yashoda: But people say all sorts of things. They point out that though your father and I both are extremely fair in complexion, you are dark in contrast. Why is it so?

Krishna: Mother it is because of you. When I was born I too was fair like you. However, it was pitch dark at that time. You were sleeping away merrily. I was sleeplessly turning sides the whole night. As a consequence, the darkness of the night stuck to me and I became black.

Krishna's simple mother could never disbelieve her son. She stretched out her hand and squeezed Him to her

Krishna

chest. The same question was put to Him insultingly by Duryodhyana, the villain of the epic Mahabharata. The following dialogue takes place there:

Duryodhyana: Nobody can say for sure who your parents are. If Nanda Baba and Yashoda are your parents then why are so black?

Krishna: I am black (kaalaa) because I have come as your end (kaal).

However, when Krishna's beloved Radha asked Him the same question, His reply was markedly different:

Radha: My Dear, Even though you are so beautiful, why are you black?

Krishna: Dear Radhe, Actually I was extremely fair. However, I have become dark only to enhance your fair beauty, which is all the more magnified by contrast with my dark complexion.

Some bhaktas speculate that since Krishna always lives in the eyes of the gopis of Vrindavana, it is the black kohl (kaajal) of their eyes that has blackened Him. Or perhaps He is dark because He absorbs all the negativity in the hearts of His worshippers.[7]

Does any of this make sense to you? Does it offend you? Does it seem like there are some obvious truths here that have been twisted beyond recognition? If it seems twisted, it's because it is. I'll explain.

Krishna was a Black god. Like many other Black gods, he is often depicted with blue skin, which was – in ancient art – considered synonymous with black.

He was depicted as Black because his myth was based on the Black gods of the indigenous Black people of India. But once whites (ancient India's Aryans) came to power, they stole these gods from the traditions they came from, and repurposed them to fit their needs. Krishna is probably the best example of this, but this happened throughout the world. To understand all this, we need to first understand how we can be so sure that Krishna was indeed a Black god.

KRISHNA'S CONNECTIONS

The name KRSNA itself means "Black." Krishna was also known by the name *Kanhaya*, which literally means "Black man."[8] The Prophet Muhammad may have recognized that Krishna was revered in India as a Black god, because a hadith records him saying, "There was a prophet of God in India who was black-skinned (*aswad al-lawn*) and his name was *Kahan*."[9] The words Kahan and Kanhaya are believed to be related.[10]

Summarizing what he'd learned in his travels across Africa and Asia, Lieutenant-Colonel James Tod connected the dots between Krishna (or *Kaniya*, the same as Kanhaya above) and the Egyptian Ramses, whom he associates with the Greek Apollo:

> Diodorus informs us that *Kan* was one of the titles of the Egyptian Apollo [Ramses]; and this is the common contraction for Kaniya. The colour of the Hindu Apollo is a dark cerulean blue (*nila*): hence he is occasionally called *Nila-Nat'h*, 'the blue god,' as well as *Sham-Nat'h*, 'the black god,' and he is invariably represented with the lotus in his hand; and like the Apollo of the Nile, Kaniya is depicted with the human form and eaglehead, one of the common hieroglyphic deities of Egypt.

Tod connects these Black Gods to the Buddhist pantheon as well:

> *Sham-nat'h* and *Shi-Nat'h*, the black divinity, are the commonest epithets of Crsna [Krishna], which name likewise means 'black.' It is curious that his cotemporary and relative *Nem-Nat'h*, the twenty-second high priest of Buddha, was also designated from his black colour, *Arisht Nemi*.[11]

In other words, all these guys had "black" in their names. Between Egypt's Ramses, the Greeks' Apollo, Hinduism's Krishna, and Buddhism's Nem-Nat'h, Tod suggests that the common thread is black skin. But who came first, and where did they come from?

Krishna

WHERE DO THESE BLACK GODS COME FROM?

Lieut. Tod asks, "Are we to bring both from the Nile, or to send them there from the Indus?" In other words, did these Black gods come from Black Egypt or did these traditions begin in Black India and work their way into the Nile Valley?

The answer seems to be a little more complicated than that. Why? These Black gods are found everywhere! In Volume Two of *Anacalypsis,* Godfrey Higgins writes:

> [T]he originals of all the Gods have been of the black race, of the class of followers of Cristna, after the black race had become improved into the shape in which we find him—that, by the handsome black males constantly uniting with the most handsome black females, their progeny increased in beauty till it arrived at the degree of perfection which we find in Cristna.

Higgins goes on to propose that the world's first government "did originally consist of this race; and that, in the East, the entire population consisting of this race, it continues black." Think about what that means for a minute.

In the West, on the other hand, Higgins says these Blacks mixed with whites, "till the whole race of the worshipers of the black God became white." In other words, some of the people who look like white folks worshipping Black folks might have originally been Black folks.

Higgins says there is no other way to explain the myths of Black Gods in Europe and China "than by supposing it carried by persons whose colour has become changed by mixture with the white inhabitants." Higgins concludes, "We have daily experience of the black races, by this process, becoming white; but we have no example of the white race going back to the black."[12]

An interesting theory to say the least, but there's quite a bit of support for it, as you'll find in Part Two of *When the World was Black.*

KRISHNA RISES TO PROMINENCE

Let's get back to Krishna. Krishna was originally not a god of great significance, but he was "selected" to become one of the great gods of Hinduism under the Aryans. As S.N. Sadasivan explains in *A Social History of India:*

> Originating from the pastoral tribes of Kathiawar, the Krishna cult through a socio-religious literature has integrated itself with the similar or parallel cults all over the country. *Mayavan* or *Karumayinira* (black colour) Kannan who was the clan god or fertility deity of the

cowherds of the south was united with the magical child, Krishna of the Bhagavata and Gopinatha, Vrijeswara, or Muralidhara of Mathura.[13]

In other words, there were many other Black gods who were revered across India, and these local deities were merged with the myth of Krishna wherever the Brahmin priesthood found it possible.

In "The Black Untouchables of India: Reclaiming our Cultural Heritage," Indian scholar V.T. Rajshekar writes, "They promoted and popularized a Black tribal hero (Krishna) and elevated him to godhood to woo back the Sudras and other masses."

Sound familiar? As you'll see in Volume Four of *The Science of Self* series, when Black populations and conquered and suppressed, their new rulers will adopt some of their indigenous icons and "repurpose" them to promote the new state religion. This is what happened with Krishna, Kali, and several other Black gods and goddesses throughout the ancient world. There's even a Black revolutionary from Palestine who later became the posterchild for the Western slave trade. Imagine that.

MAYON, A NATIVE BLACK GOD

Earlier, we mentioned some of the local Black gods who were absorbed under the worship of Krishna. In other cases, these older gods were said to be the same as newer Brahmin deities who had similar traits. For example, the authors of the Bhagavata attempt to "integrate the southern pastoral or fertility deity Mayon (the black) with the child god of Gokula in Kathiawar and the adolescent romantic hero dwelling in Vrindavana."[14] The similarity between them made it easy to say that Mayon was really no different from these minor characters, and that the worship of Mayon should cease so that the "real" Brahmin gods could take over.

Who was Mayon? In his *History of the Tamils*, P.T. Srinivasa Iyengar tells us that Mayon was no minor character:

> The god of the pastoral region – Mullai – was the Black God (Mayon), who was a herdsman, beloved of both milkmaids and of cattle. He was always uttering sweet music with the flute, and its music moved all nature. Besides singing, he delighted in dancing. Surrounded by a crowd of milkmaids, he or his priest danced most complicated dances, as herdsfolk do today.

Mayon was also reputed to be a renowned lover, and was considered to live the ideal life for the herdsman who revered him. Ivengar concludes, "Hence the Black God of the tenders of cattle is the jolliest of the Indian gods."[15]

Much of Mayon's mythology was incorporated into the story of Krishna. However, rather than being a "jolly" exemplar for the pastoral communities where Mayon was worshipped across southern India, Krishna was now a representative for the brutality of Brahmanism, the oppressive "state" religion of the Aryans who had taken over.

THE REAL KRISHNA

In Winthrop Sargeant's book on *The Bhagavad Gita*, he details the story of Krishna as it was told in the Hindu scriptures. In short, we learn how his story was interwoven with the mythology associated with Mayon, giving him the authenticity of an indigenous Black god. But the god of the *Bhagavad Gita* was a warrior (like the Aryans), and he killed nearly every indigenous god he encountered! The only thing Black about this Krishna was his name!

Whatever the original Krishna was about, you wouldn't find it in the *Bhagavad Gita*. You'll find stories of Mayon mixed with stories of a ruthless Aryan warrior, fighting for white rule in India. Countless native gods and warriors attempted to stop him, but all of them failed. It wasn't until the armies of Jarasamdha, King of Maghada, combined forces with those of Kalayavana, a "Black Greek," that Krishna was forced to abandon his stronghold in Mathura, fleeing to the gated city of Dvaraka, where he was safe behind its stone walls.[16]

THE SWITCH

Throughout ancient history, two traditions competed for dominance: the unseen God in heaven, who authorized the power of the ruling class, and the Black god (on Earth) who symbolized the common people. That is, the anthropomorphized Black god represented the ancestors of the people, while the unseen (and presumably white) God represented the "invisible hand" of the elite.

Nearly every civilization and religion of the ancient world has its own Black male deities. Yet, with the rise of whites to power, which happened across the world, this Black god was quickly co-opted, and repurposed as the voice of the new elite and their orthodoxy. Thus, although it took thousands of years for the "collective self" of the Indian people to become personified as the Black God Krishna, it would only take a few hundred years for the invading Aryans to turn the same Krishna into the posterboy for Hinduism and their racially oppressive caste system.

WHY WAS KALI BLACK?

"William Jones remarks also that the remains of ancient art in India as well as the statues of the Hindoo Gods, appear to have been modelled on the African rather than the Hindoo type. The black woolly-haired tribes of the Andamans are negroes beyond dispute, and the hypothesis that these tribes which are also found in the interior of the Malay peninsula, are the relics of a people once extensively spread over Central Asia, does not appear by any means improbable." – Notes and Queries on China and Japan, 1867

Kali

Kali is the Hindu goddess of time and change. Kālī is the feminine form of kālam, meaning "black." Her name means "the black one" and she is always depicted with black skin.

However, there's quite some debate about why, with many scholars suggesting that her blackness is symbolic of death, time, or the night sky.

We know that many of India's deities have black skin or black faces. But, as noted in the quote above, this wasn't simply some "aesthetic" thing. Nor was it entirely symbolic of the heavens, the night sky, the fertile soil, or the underworld.

Sometimes, those things were a part of their mythology, but many of these deities were notably "Africoid" in their earliest depictions. In other words, they didn't start out as abstract concepts who were "assigned" a Black color. They were Black men and women who were assigned divine status.

Agni, God of Fire

Thus Kali is not painted black simply because of her association with death. Instead, Kali was probably one of the "old guard" of India's deities who survived the Aryan conquest and was absorbed into the Hindu pantheon. In the Mundaka Upanishad, Kali is named as one of the seven tongues of Agni, the Hindu god of fire. In the oldest statues, Agni is depicted with African features.

Rama

GREAT GOD RAMA

Rama is the seventh avatar of the Supreme God Vishnu, and a king of Ayodhya in Hindu scriptures. Rama is one of the most important avatars of Vishnu (Krishna was the eighth), and one of the most popular gods in Hinduism. He is widely worshipped throughout Nepal and India, sometimes as a Supreme God himself.

As S.N. Sadasivan explains in *A Social History of India*, "pastoral gods or fertility deities all over India were of dark complexion, which they sung as irresistibly beautiful and religiously auspicious." In other words, the holiest and most beautiful way to be was Black.

Sadasivan continues, noting that high god Rama was most certainly a Black god:

> The seductive charm of the black complexion has been the object of floral adoration of southern poets from ancient times and the Ramayana itself extols the ecstatic beauty of Rama's dark colour.[17]

VISHNU, THE SUPREME GOD

Vishnu is a major god in Hindu mythology. He is seen as the preserver of the universe, while two other major gods, Brahma and Shiva, are its creator and destroyer. Vishnu is portrayed as black or blue, with four arms symbolizing different the functions he serves.

Like Krishna, he may have begun as a local Black god who later became a major part of the state religion. It is believed that Vishnu was a god who came to Earth (as an avatar) to keep things in order, and that ten incarnations (or reincarnations) of Vishnu would occur. Rama and Krishna were said to be the seventh and eighth of these incarnations, with the tenth yet to come.

Himalayan Image of Shiva

A CELEBRATION OF BLACKNESS?

There's certainly a lot of blackness in the oldest traditions of India. But why do so many Indians have such negative ideas about black skin?

As you may know, my family hails from Bangladesh (once a part of

India, until the British came). I've seen firsthand how the majority of our people have dark skin and even some African features, yet many of us have serious issues with color and class (or caste).[18]

Historian Pranab Chatergee has written about how Bengali culture has approached the issue of Black skin:

> Traditionally, in European and American cultures, the color black often takes on a derogatory meaning. First, being black or dark skinned often reduces one to a lesser status in society. Second, the languages pick up this attribution and mirror the prejudices of the culture. For example, the usages, blackball, black market, black book, blacklist, etc. mean that black is not desirable. On the other hand, whiteness is associated with honesty, beauty, and desirability.
>
> Bengali culture, however, is caught in a similar conflict between blackness and whiteness. On one hand, perhaps because of having Caucasian ancestors in the remote past and of living under a white nation's rule, whiteness is preferred and even valued. However, because of the colossal presence of Krishna and his legacy, and because many native Bengali men and women are dark-skinned, a tradition of celebrating blackness has also emerged. In the European languages, such a tradition of celebrating blackness is relatively rare.
>
> Later the Bengali poet, Rabindranath Thakur (1861-1941) would borrow from the Vaishnab tradition. He has many poems with metaphors like "tender as the black night," "they call her black, I call her black tulip," "awesome black, like this universe, with some stars here and there," "in your black eyes is reflected the shadow of rain," or "engulf me like a black night." Many other contemporary and classical Bengali poets and musicians are openly celebratory about being black, being in the company of persons who are black, and of a surrender to a Black God.

Sounds great, doesn't it? This "celebration of Blackness" does not, however, always translate into meaningful behavior.

Chatergee continues:

> It should be noted, however, that there are contradictions that coexist here. These contradictions are between verbal and non-verbal behavior. At the verbal level, many Bengali persons assert that a dark-skinned girl's beauty should be appreciated, and that a dark skinned man's dignity should be socially supported. All this is said but often not done. At the non-verbal level, one sees matrimonial ads openly requiring fair-skinned brides. And in both Bengals, a white man (*sahib*) or a white woman (*mem-sahib*) is immediately treated with high status. Such conferring of status may be due to the legacy of a culture that was ruled by white men and women (the British) until recently.[19]

Sound familiar? It should. All over the world, the same struggle.

AN INTRODUCTION TO BUDDHISM

Buddha - Thailand

Buddhism is another tradition that originated in ancient India. Across the world, there are over 300 million people who follow its various sects.

Most people date the birth of Buddhism to the time of Siddhartha Gautama, a prince born into the Indian nobility around the 6th century BC. Gautama is said to have left his family's palace, where he discovered suffering, struggle, desire, and deception. He dedicated himself to understanding the root of these problems, and his path of discovery led him to enlightenment.

From this time forward, he became a Buddha, which is not a name, but a title he was given. The name is derived from the word "budhi," which means "to awaken." The Buddha then went about India, teaching others. His followers soon spread far and wide, developing a variety of sects, some of which later spread into the Far East.

THE "NEGRO" BUDDHA

But who was the Buddha? In *Anacalypsis*, British historian Godfrey Higgins suggests that Buddha descended from the aboriginal "Negroes" of ancient India:

> The mountaineers [of India] most resemble Negroes in their countenances and their hair. The natives of the hilly districts of Bengal and Bahar can hardly be distinguished by their features from the modern Ethiopians." All this accords very well with my theory respecting the black Buddha. It has been observed that the figures in all the old caves of India have the appearance of Negroes. This tends to prove not only the extreme antiquity of the caves but also the original Negro character of the natives.[20]

Siddharta Gautama - Buddhist Cave Fresco

In Crooke's study of Krishna, he connects the Blackness of Buddha, the Tibetan Lamas, and the Black people who must have established these precedents:

> Now it has been often noticed that some of the forms of the Indian Buddha and other black Hindu gods are of a distinctively negroid type, representing the deity with thick lips, long hanging ear lobes, and black curly hair which cannot be referred to any existing Indian people.

> Dr. Waddell describes the Lama of Tibet as a man with short curly hair, like the conventional images of Buddha; the courtiers depicted in the rock paintings of the Ajanta caves have fair or dark brown curly hair, while the attendants are black with curly negroid hair, and some are dwarfs; the images of the Jaina saint Gautama have crisp curly hair, thick lips, and black skin. The enlargement of the ear lobe has also been often noticed.

Crooke concludes, "It may be suspected that in these representations we have a proof of negroid or negrito influence on Indian religious beliefs."

WAS THERE MORE THAN ONE BUDDHA?

Were the above scholars talking about Siddharta Gautama or the Buddhas who came before him?

It's quite likely that Siddhartha was dark-skinned with woolly hair, as many South Indians still carry these features even today. But it should be noted that Buddhist traditions say that Siddhartha was not the first Buddha, but rather one of many, in a long line of succession. Some accounts suggest that Siddhartha was instructed by the Buddha who came before him.

In Jainism, it is widely accepted that the Buddha was taught by Jains. Enlightened men, in Jain tradition, are known as Tirthankaras and Arihants. Such figures were often made into large statues by Jains in India, and these statues look a lot like the Black Buddhas.

Thus, the depictions of the Black Buddha – found throughout India, Sri Lanka, Japan, China, Tibet, Cambodia, Vietnam, and Thailand – may not all depict Siddhartha Gautama, but some of the "other" Buddhas as well. The Buddhas who came before Siddharta could have been more "Africoid" than Siddharta himself.

What we know for sure is that all of the oldest representations of Buddha, Siddharta or otherwise, show that the Buddha was a Black man. It's only after Buddhism had been long established in other parts of Asia that he gradually began to be portrayed with East Asian features.

Buddha - Cambodia

Buddhist Cave Fresco

A Jain icon, possibly Mahavira

An Introduction to Jainism

Dating back to at least 877 BC (but most likely much older), Jainism is one of the oldest religions still active today. For long stretches, Jainism was the state religion of India and was widespread across south Asia, but today it's down to about four million adherents. It's important because it's not simply ancient, but its traditions predate both modern Hinduism and modern Buddhism. That is, Jainism may be the name by which we should know what Buddhism was like before Siddharta Gautama.

In fact, Prince Siddharta studied under Jains during his six years of wandering before becoming the Buddha. If he was, indeed, taught by a Buddha before him, that individual may have been recognized by the Jains, who teach of a succession of enlightened men who teach the world. Like ancient Buddhism, however, Jainism doesn't teach of a personal God or Creator. Instead, it is a highly metaphysical tradition with a much more "science of self" approach to the universe. Jains believe their tradition to be eternal, with no beginning or ending, only being occasionally forgotten by humans and revived by a succession of enlightened teachers.

In Jainism, anyone can be enlightened and "godliness" or perfection is an inherent quality of one who has "perfect knowledge, perfect peace, infinite bliss, and infinite power." Jains teach that several especially enlightened individuals have emerged throughout history to teach and direct the course of humanity. These divine beings are known as Arihantas and Tīrthankaras, the closest characters we'll find to the "gods" of Jainism.

RISHABHA, THE FIRST TIRTHANKARA

Arihantas are humans who have achieved enlightenment and great

Rishabha

power, while the Tīrthankaras are the Arihantas who lead and teach others. There are 24 Tīrthankaras in each time cycle. The first is Rishabha, who is credited for organizing India's people from indigenous foragers into a settled urban society. He introduced a total of 72 sciences, including mathematics, law, writing, ceramics, textiles, metallurgy, and agriculture, as well as the art of lovemaking, singing, and dancing.

Indian scholars suggest that Rishabha, also known as Adeshvara ("Primal Lord"), may have lived in the era when the Indus

Valley civilization emerged. According to Gupta, Rishabha's kingdom existed during the time of Mohenjo-Daro and Harappa, around 3000 BC.[21] Rankin, on the other hand, dates him back to the first urban society in the region, circa 7000 BC.[22]

These scholars connect Rishabha with a god depicted on seals in the ancient Indus Valley. This figure often wears the head of a bull and sits or stands in a yoga posture. Some scholars believe the Hindu god Shiva was derived from this ancient god.

Rishabha was most likely one of the Black leaders of ancient India. He is typically portrayed with the African features we find in the artwork from those periods. Rishabha's son, Bahubali, who is revered as an Arihant, also looks very "Negroid" in most of the massive statues erected across India to commemorate him.

In fact, many of the most important Jain Arihantas and Tirthankaras are sculpted to look like Black men. "These representations," Crooke says, are "proof of negroid or negrito influence on Indian religious beliefs."

BAHUBALI, SON OF RISHABHA

A 1900 study cites a Jain statue in South Kanara having African features from head to toe, quite literally from the curls of his hair to the length of his limbs:

> Remarkable it is, too, that the features show nothing distinctively Hindu. The hair grows in close crisp curls; the broad fleshy cheeks might make the face seem heavy, were it not for the marked and dignified expression conferred by the calm forward gazing eyes and aquiline nose, somewhat pointed at tip. The forehead is of average size, the lips very

Bahubali - Dharmasthala

full and thick, the upper one long almost to ugliness, throwing the chin, though full and prominent, into the shade. The arms, which touch the body only at the hips, are remarkably long, the large, well-formed hands and fingers reaching to the knees.[23]

The statue described above was most likely the 35-foot-tall statue of Bahubali (also known as Gomateshwara).

PARSVANATHA, THE 23ᴿᴰ TIRTHANKARA

Pārśvanātha (877-777 BC) was the 23rd Tirthankara of Jainism, and the earliest Jain leader accepted as a historical figure. He is the most "loved" among Jain adherents. He too, is depicted with Africoid features. Sometimes, he is entirely black, except for his teeth and the whites of his eyes.

Parsvanatha

MAHAVIRA, THE LAST TIRTHANKARA

Mahāvīra (540-463 BC) was the 24th and last Tīrthankara of the current time cycle. He was one of the most popular teachers to spread Jainism, but he's regarded as a "reformer" rather than its founder. His statues often look like those of the Black Buddha.

Icons of Mahavira

Take a break.
Put this book down for a minute.

Do NOT go back to reading this book until you do one (or more) of the following things:

- ❑ Call somebody who is going through some rough sh*t and make sure they are okay.
- ❑ Eat something that your body is telling you it needs, or drink some water.
- ❑ Wrestle, spar, or slapbox someone to make sure you "still got it."
- ❑ Take a walk through your neighborhood and see if somebody needs help with something.
- ❑ Clean up a part of your house, or organize some f*cked up part of your life.
- ❑ Tell somebody about this book and what you're learning. Invite them to come read it.
- ❑ Give this book away to somebody who needs it and get another copy for yourself.
- ❑ Cook something good, and make enough to share. Invite people.
- ❑ Check yourself out in the mirror and pick something to improve.
- ❑ Identify ten positive things about your life and stop forgetting them when you're stressed.
- ❑ Tell somebody you love them, cause it might be your last chance.

This has been a PSA from 360 and SDP.
Once you're done, carry on.

THE BLACK GOD OF SRI LANKA

A GOD BECOMES A DEVIL

The *Yakkun nattannawā* is a Cingalese poem from ancient Sri Lanka, an island just south of India which was once known as Ceylon. This tradition begins:

> To the supreme Budha named Lowtura, and to his doctrines and priests, I make obeisance. The greater One is God! The goddesses named Pattinees will ever protect us, and all men...In the island of Black Marble, beyond the Seven Seas, a golden palace was erected. The Queen that was in the palace, named Karandoo Bana, or the Fishing Baskets, conceived; and, ten months after, brought forth a son...He was conceived in the pure womb of Karandoo Bana; and was born with influence and power...Having discovered a lucky time, they gave him food in the seventh month. From thence the name of this great prince was, the Great Black God.

The tradition, which seems to have been fragmented and reassembled, continues:

> He grew from day to day; he shone like the full moon; and, accompanied by the god Riddee, reconnoitred [surveyed, in a military sense] every place. He received power from the god Riddee, and came to the world of men, and...causeth the people who behold him to be sick; he having pleasantly descended into seven lakes, his hair being purified with lemon-juice, and his person decorated.

> O thou Great Black God, take away the sickness of this person!...There is no other god besides thee in the midst of the sixteen hundred queens. Thou seizest men, and causest them to be sick by placing them in solitude. We have accordingly prepared sweetmeats, and offered them to thee without any mistake. O thou Great Black God, preserve the sick person by cheering him![24]

The belief that this God had power over sickness, death, and healing was transformed into one that demonizes him as only being the source of sickness. From this time forward, the "Great Black God" became associated with the "Devil Prince" and later, a "Black Devil."

When did this change occur? If other areas provide any clue, it most likely occurred when European missionaries and political leaders began stepping into Sri Lanka.

THE BLACK GODS OF CHINA

Most people would consider China an unlikely place to find Black gods. Yet, throughout China's earliest history, there's considerable reverence to figures who look unmistakably Black.

In the period BEFORE we have any record of traditional Chinese religion, we find artifacts and artwork from the shamanic traditions of the indigenous Chinese. And whenever we start looking at indigenous traditions, we find something or someone who looks much more African than the people and traditions that came later.

THE HIGH GOD OF THE SHANG DYNASTY

The Xia and Shang dynasties were the foundational dynasties of ancient Chinese civilization. Before then, the people of the region were clustered in communities that were not organized. Thus there was no state religion. By the time of the Shang, however, there was widespread recognition of a High God, known originally as *Di* (or *Ti*), then later as *Shang Di*, which some authors translate as "the lord above."[25]

They also revered lesser deities representing natural forces. One example was *Tu*, the 'Earth Power,' or the "Altar of the Soil."[26] A number of such divinities, as well as important totems such as the black bird, played a significant role as early as the Neolithic period, and continued to do so into the Shang period.[27]

According to Wolfram Eberhard:

> The supreme god of official worship was called Shang Di; he was a god of vegetation who guided all growth and birth and was later conceived of as a forefather of the races of mankind. The earth was represented as a mother goddess, who bore the plants and animals procreated by Shang Di. In some parts of the Shang realm the two were conceived as a married couple who later were parted by one of their children. The husband went to heaven and the rain is the male seed that creates life on earth.[28]

The name of the high God, Di, was used by the Shang kings to address their royal ancestors and deceased kings, who also occupied a space in the cosmic hierarchy of the ancient religion.[29] According to one author, the first Shang king was called *Xuan Wang*, or "Black King," and alternately *Xuan Di*, or "Black Emperor."[30] Xuan Di may also be translated "Black God." The name *Di* was later used by living rulers during the Warring States period.[31]

Modern Chinese Shaman

WHAT ARE SHAMANS?

What was Chinese religion like before the Xia and Shang dynasties? Like indigenous societies elsewhere in the world, they didn't have a state religion run by a priesthood. Instead, they had shamans.

The shaman, in the earliest periods, was not only the chief religious figure, but the chief social/political figure as well. The roles of leader, teacher, healer, and shaman were often one and the same. These shamans were also indigenous scientists. Chinese historian K.C. Chang has said that the shamans of ancient times were "mathematicians who understood heaven and earth and were sages and wise men."[32] According to Keightley, the shamans of the Shang dynasty were "combining pyromancy with another form of divination that employed the manipulation of numbers." This is where the Chinese oracle system known as the *I-Ching* comes from.

Everywhere we find the earliest instances of shamanism, even in China, we find people who look Black. For example, there are ancient bronze tetrapods (three-legged containers) and jade *cong* (ritual artifacts) associated with shamanic rituals. These often feature characters with large, round eyes, thick lips, wide noses, and coarse or woolly hair.

One Shang dynasty tetrapod, depicts a male shaman with his animal alter-ego, a tiger. The shaman is clearly a small-statured Black man, often described as a "Negrito." As there's no accepted "group name" for these people throughout the world, I call them the DBP (or Diminutive Black People).

As DBP communities are typically the oldest human populations wherever they are found, shamanism – which is older than most ancient religions – is a DBP tradition. Of the DBP in Asia, Logan notes:

> We find in these [Negrito] tribes a pure Shamanism with its accompaniment of charms and talismans. This is a living faith, dating from the remotest times in Asia, which has preserved its original simplicity and vigor, unspoiled by either Buddhism or Mohammedanism.[33]

These people were considered the holiest and most powerful people of the ancient world, and China was no exception to this rule. Art historian James Brunson theorized:

> The prominent role of the Africoid type in Shang art suggests intriguing possibilities in the realm of political power...If so many ritualistic works depict the Africoid type, one must recognize the authority of blacks during the Shang period, if not earlier.[34]

Much of this is corroborated by the results of several scholars' analyses of the more than 120 diviners (or shamans) who served the last nine Shang kings. Out of ten groups, sorted chronologically, the *Huang* ("yellow") group is the absolute latest, making its appearance in the reign of King Wen Ding (1116-1106 B.C.).

Two varieties of the *Li* ("black") group predate the *Huang*. In fact, excluding the periods where a "Nameless" group was predominant or the major group is unknown, the "black" shamans make up the majority in all of the kings' reigns before the *Huang* come.[35]

THE BLACK IMMORTALS

Most historians don't say much about the "little Black people" of ancient China. Chinese anthropologist Li Chi notes a reference to "blackish-colored dwarfs" in the *Official History of the Liang Dynasty* (502–556 AD),[36] but comes up short for other references in early Chinese literature.

I'm not sure how he missed it, but the Chinese actually have a rich literary and artistic tradition centered on these indigenous Black people, who may have been the direct descendants of China's first settlers. Somehow, after first reaching the area over 50,000 years ago, these people survived well into recent times. They didn't maintain large communities, but the mere fact that ANY of them survived is a testament to who and what they were.

Thus, when we do find records of their presence, the stories are remarkable and sound like myths and legends. For starters, *Kunlun Nu* ("The Negrito Slave") is a popular Chinese romance written during the Tang Dynasty around 880 AD. The hero of the tale is a

"Negrito" slave named *Mo-lê*, who has "supernatural" physical abilities.

After Mo-lê saves his master's lover (who has now fallen for him), he finally escapes with his dagger (apparently his only possession). He literally flies over the city walls to escape apprehension. This small but legendary Black man is seen over ten years later, selling medicine in the city, not having aged a single day.

Later Taoist commentary says that Mo-lê's gravity-defying abilities and agelessness suggest he was a Chinese Immortal (a mythical group popular in early Taoism and modern Kung fu movies).[37] In fact, it appears that the "Immortals" of Chinese tradition were inspired by stories of these "magical" Blacks, much as the stories of the mythical beings of Europe's "enchanted forests" were based on the ancient Black presence there.

For example, according to Taoist adept Ge Hong, some hunters in the Zhongnan Mountains saw a naked man whose body – from a distance – appeared to be covered in black hair. In other words, he was black all over. Whenever they tried to capture him he "leapt over gullies and valleys as if in flight, and so could not be overtaken."[38] Sounds like the stuff of legend. But these were real people.

It is from such legendary Black people that myths and religions are born. Such mysterious individuals were often the founders of important traditions, many of which became local cults and religions. Until the time when they could no longer be found, they often played important roles as shamans or medicine men, as we've noted above.

By the time state religions become widespread in later years, we still find some record of the Black men and women who founded them, but they are much more enshrouded in myth and symbolic language.

Fu Xi and Nu Kua

THE THREE AUGUST ONES

Traditional Chinese history begins with the age of the Three August Ones (*San Huang*). They were Fu Xi, Nu Kua and Shen Nung.[39] These three symbolized the origins of the Chinese people.

Fu Xi, the head of this trinity, was originally depicted as a Black god.[40] His wife Nu Kua was depicted similarly. The third member of the *San Huang,* Shen Nung, was said to have had the head of a black ox, which might have referred to either a physical attribute or a totemic idea.[41] Like Shen Nung, one of the early Shang dynasty emperors is said to have been called *Xuan mu,* or "Black Ox."

NU KUA AND THE MAKING OF MAN

Nu Kua was seen as both the wife and sister of Fu Xi.[42] This wasn't a literal thing, but symbolic of the intertwined nature of the masculine and feminine elements of creation. Thus, Fu Xi and Nu Kua were often drawn connected by means of a tail or with their lower bodies intertwined like serpents. Later tales assigned her a role in the creation mythology, saying:

> There were no men when the sky and the earth were separated. It was Nu Wa [Nu Kua] who made men by molding yellow clay. The work was so taxing that her strength was not equal to it. So she dipped a rope into the mud and then lifted it. The mud that dripped from the rope also became men. Those made by moulding yellow clay were rich and noble, while those made by lifting the rope were poor and low.[43]

In other words, the dark-skinned "mud people" became China's "common people," while the higher class was made from bright yellow clay. Sounds racist huh? But it makes sense when you consider the historical context that produced this myth.

This is what happened under the Zhou, a foreign population who took over China and created a new class of light-skinned privilege and nobility. What matters to us is that, while the "yellow" people belonged to the privileged aristocracy, the common people, who were by far the established (and indigenous) majority, were dark brown, or black, like the mud of prehistoric Chinese soil.[44] How did this happen? The story is told in myth.

47

THE NEW ZHOU RELIGION

In traditional Chinese mythology, after the age of the San Huang follows the Age of Five Sovereigns (*Wu Di*). These were Huang Ti, Zhuan Xu, Shun, Yao, and Yu.[45] It's this second batch of deities, particularly Huang Ti (or "Yellow God") who are associated with the origins of the "yellow Chinese."

How did this change occur? According to one account:

> After Shun [the last Sovereign] there succeeded Yu, who founded Xia, and when Xia became perverted the Yin [Shang] destroyed them and took their place. The Zhou at last drove out the Yin [Shang] when they became evil-doers.[46]

In other words, the Zhou ultimately conquered the indigenous people of China, doing as most conquerers do, and saying their predecessors were "evil" and had to be unseated from power. The foreign Zhou said they were descended "both from Huang-ti and from K'i, son of Heaven and a Virgin Mother, who had acquired merit in the reign of Shun as Minister of Agriculture and Prince of the Harvests."[47]

The Zhou – who had invaded from the west soon after the Aryans invaded India – in turn claimed exclusive right to the title of king, as well as authority over the worship of a high God, *Tian* (or *T'ien*), of whom they called themselves sons (*Tian tzu*, that is, "son of Heaven").[48] Sound familiar? A conquering people naming themselves the children of God as a means to claim their right to unquestionable power?

So this was the beginning of an abstract, transcendental god in the heavens. This invisible "Father in Heaven" idea wasn't promoted because it was a great spiritual idea, but because it solidified the power of the conquering class. Before this, the gods of ancient China were quite human…and often quite Black.

PAN GU, THE ORIGINAL MAN

Because China is such a large place, where so many communities have come together, sharing and trading traditions, Chinese traditional religion has a large pantheon of deities, like those in Greece, Rome, Egypt, Mexico, West Africa, and India. And just as in other places, one Chinese community might worship a different set of gods from another community on the other side of the mountains.

In some traditions, the first of the gods was Pan Gu, who was both the "original man" and the original of all man. Xu Zheng, in the early third century A.D., wrote of this primal deity who made the heavens and earth into their current form[49]:

> First born was Pan Gu, who as he was moribund [near death] became transformed. [His] breath became the wind and the clouds; his voice became the thunder; his left eye became the sun, and his right eye became the moon...his sweat became rain and lakes; and the various worms in his body, touched by the wind, became the black-haired commoners.[50]

It's intriguing to take note of the parallels between this myth and the creation myths of many African and Near Eastern cosmologies, where the first man not only fathers all people, but his actual body becomes the world itself. We should also look at that reference to "black-haired commoners" in this primordial period. As I explained in *When the World was Black*, such descriptions were originally not about hair color, but the color of one's "head."

Many scholars have said that Pan Gu, identified a the first man, was originally a god of southern Chinese peoples and only later became widespread.[51] Wolfram Eberhard clarifies in his compilation *Folktales of China* that Pan Gu was connected specifically with the aboriginal societies of the south.[52] In other words, the dark-skinned people who first established Chinese civilization were the ones who spread the story of Pan Gu, the original man.

A separate myth describes Pan Gu making men out of clay. These first men had become "baked by the rays of the sun," until storm clouds forced Pan Gu to sweep them into the house.[53] This may allude, again, to the dark skin of the early Chinese, who like the Ethiopians, appeared to have been "burnt by the sun."

THE ORIGIN OF ALL

Eberhard says the Pan Gu mythos, specifically the account of the "world-egg" from which the primeval god was born, was quite ancient, dating back at least to the Shang dynasty, if not older.[54] In this tradition, Pan Gu emerged from a primordial egg, wherein there laid dormant the sky and the earth. He then separated the two, a process that took eighteen thousand years.

Somewhere between sky and earth, Pan Gu transformed himself, going through "nine changes a day," performing "like a god in Heaven and like a sage on Earth,"[55] for another eighteen thousand years, until finally, the world was primed for the coming of the Three

Emperors. These were the Emperor of the Sky, the Emperor of the Earth, and the Emperor of Men, a triumvirate which corresponds to that of the Three August Ones. Pan Gu, in this process, became both man and mathematics.

Thus, the myth continues: "So these numbers came into existence and evolve like this. The number begins with one, becomes established at three, is completed at five, prospers at seven, and ends in nine."[56] This numerical symbolism, where the 1-9 procession is used to describe the development of the universe, is found everywhere from the *Tao te Ching* to the *Kabbalah*. It is, in fact, a useful (and accurate) way to explain some very complicated science, as we explain in *The Science of Self, Volume One*. In a future title, we'll explore this teaching in depth.

Several isolated Negrito peoples in Southeast Asia recount a similar mythos. For example, in the origin legend of the Andamanese Aka-Bo, it is said: "The first man was Jutpu [means "alone"]. He was born inside the joint of a big bamboo, just like a bird in an egg. The bamboo split and he came out. He was a little child."

The myth continues, as in the Chinese tradition, that the Creator deity and first man, Jutpu, grew larger and larger, building larger huts for himself each time he grew. After molding woman from a lump of clay, he made other people (the ancestors, called *tomo-la*), and taught them in turn.

In short, the original man created the universe before the development of man himself, and then became the original of all men. These men are, of course, described as Black. The Andaman Aka-Jeru people's myth is almost exactly the same.[57]

THE BLACK BIRD AND THE EGG

Wherever you find ancient evidence of Black people, you'll find a creation myth involving a black bird and a cosmic egg. The egg myth is also found in the history of ancient China. A tradition recorded by Sima Qian in the *Shi Ji* (*Historical Record*, circa 90 B.C.) states that Qi, the Shang progenitor (circa 2300-2200 B.C.) was born from the egg of a black bird.[58]

The *Yen Ben Zhi*, too, records that the Shang dynasty founder was born to a woman named Jian Di who, upon going with two others to take a bath, "saw that a black bird dropped an egg. Jian Di took and devoured it, became impregnated and gave birth to Xieh [Qi]."[59]

A Shang poem, entitled *Xuan Niao* (literally "Black Bird"), recounts:

"Heaven bade the dark bird/ to come down and bear Shang,"[60] while the Shi Jing records an identical tradition: "To the people of Shang, heaven ordered the black bird to descend and to give birth."[61]

People may not have worshipped these black birds, but the cosmic power they symbolized (the origin of all humanity) should not be ignored. Also, what color would the beings born from the egg of a black bird be?

KUAN TI AND CHANG FEI

Kuan Ti is a god revered across East Asia, where he is respected by Buddhists, Taoists, and Confucianists alike. Considered to have great power over demons, he was given a wealth of titles, such as "Prayer Answering Illustrious King," "Brave Peace Bringing King," "Warrior Prince and Civilizer," and even "Supreme Ruler of the Universe." Kinda like a Chinese Five Percenter.

This "God of War" did not do his work alone, however. Kuan Ti was associated with two other gods, Chang Fei and Liu Bei. Sidney Gamble writes:

> These three were specially noted for their unsurpassed loyalty. They were worshiped by those swearing brotherhood. Together they protected the district and kept it peaceful as Kuan Ti's big sword chased away the demons, Liu Pei's two edged sword had power over poisonous insects, and Chang Fei's spear gave prosperity.

The god with the spear, Chang Fei, was said to have "a black face with big eyes like the stars."[62] In many statues, Kuan Ti is also shown having a dark brown complexion.

These Black gods were not entirely mythical, however. Kuan Ti (also written as Guan Di) was once a general serving under the warlord Liu Bei in the late Eastern Han Dynasty of China (206 BC – 220 AD). He played a significant role in the civil war that led to the collapse of the Han Dynasty and the establishment of the state of Shu Han in the Three Kingdoms period, of which Liu Bei was the first emperor.

As one of the best known Chinese historical figures throughout East

Asia, his stories were passed down through oral tradition. The embellished stories can be found in novels like *Romance of the Three Kingdoms*, in which his deeds and moral qualities have been made legendary.

Kuan Ti was respected as an epitome of loyalty and righteousness, and was deified as early as the Sui Dynasty (581–618 AD). He is still worshipped by many Chinese people today, especially in southern China, Taiwan, Hong Kong, and among many overseas Chinese communities.

Kuan Ti, Chang Fei, and Liu Bei

BODHIDHARMA

Bodhidharma is the founder of Zen Buddhism in China. Some scholars also say he established the Shaolin school of martial arts, where he is also known as *Da-mo* (from *Dharma*, a Buddhist concept).

Bodhidharma

Born in Southern India, early artwork depicts him as dark-skinned, with a wide nose and often woolly hair. He's not technically considered a god, but there are many legendary stories told about him, especially among adherents of Zen Buddhism. He's considered "semi-divine."

CONFUCIUS

Confucius was the founder of Confucianism, a philosophy that grew to epic proportions in ancient China. Confucius focused on the relationships and responsibilities of humans rather than the affairs of the gods. Yet Confucius himself was elevated to a semi-divine status by his later adherents.

We don't know much about the historical Confucius, so we shouldn't jump to labeling him as "Black" without strong evidence. However, early accounts of Confucius describe him as ugly or dark. Across Asia, there are quite a few paintings and statues that depict him with dark skin.

Statue of Confucius - Taiwan

LAO TZU

Like Confucius, we don't know much about the historical Lao Tzu, who composed the *Tao te Ching* and founded Taoism around the 4th century B.C. It would be safe to assume that, if Lao Tzu was a historical personality, he would look like other Chinese men of his time. There are, however, shrines that commemorate Lao Tzu as a dark-skinned man.

Buddha, Lao Tzu, Confucius (Japan)

CAI-SHEN

Cai-shen is the god of prosperity in Taoism and Chinese folk religion. He has various powers, such as preventing bad weather, and ensuring that businesses do well. Micha F. Lindemans writes:

> Cai-shen is usually portrayed riding on a black tiger. He has a black face and a thick moustache. On his head he wears a cap made of iron and he holds a weapon, also made of iron.[63]

As a god of prosperity, Cai-shen may have been like Ekchuah, the Mayan god of traders and travelling merchants, or like Daikoku, one of the seven "lucky" gods of the Japanese.

WHAT IS CHI?

Chi is one of the East Asian concepts of "spirit" or "energy" that can be found in humans. Like the Hebrew *ruakh*, the Egyptian *ka*, or the Igbo (Nigerian) concept also known as *chi*, this energy represents the way in which humans are connected to the divine.

---

* An excerpt from *The Hidden Tradition*, also from Supreme Design Publishing.

It's something like saying the omnipotent force that created this universe is an ocean, and we are cups of ocean water. We contain within us the same potential. Thus, in Chinese tradition, *chi* is seen as a great power that can be used to heal, transform, and accomplish what might otherwise seem impossible.

THE BLACK GODS OF JAPAN

In the 1500s, few Europeans had explored Japan, much less written about it to tell others. In 1602, Marcelo de Ribadeneira published one of the first European accounts of Japanese religion and culture.

Shakyamuni Buddha

THE BLACK GODS AMIDA AND XACA

As we might expect, Ribadeneira's account is hostile and shallow. What's notable, however, is that he calls the Japanese an "idol-loving" people who worship a large number of gods, the most important of which are Amida and "the black god Xaca."

Ribadeneira says both gods were once men, perhaps rulers of kingdoms. He is partly right. "Xaca" refers to Shakyamuni Buddha, widely considered the "Supreme Buddha" in most schools of Buddhism.

Amida also refers to a Buddha, Amitābha Buddha, the principal figure in the Pure Land sect, a branch of Buddhism popular in Japan. Amitābha is also recognized in other sects of Buddhism. Most traditions trace him back to the monk Dharmakara, who studied and became a bodhisattva, and eventually a Buddha.

Ribadeneira discusses the significance of the Buddhist priests and nuns who lead these sects, but their theology is clearly different from the traditions of the West. He says their sects emphasize meditation and the discipline of the mind and will, rather than prayer and submission. "Heaven," he reports, "is interior peace, while Hell is inquietude, anxiety, due to an undisciplined mind and will, and a heart full of desires and afflicted by mundane cares."

It would make sense that when Buddha was imported to Japan, he was still revered as Black. However, Buddhism was only introduced to Japan around 538 A.D. What about before then? As it turns out, Japan had, and still has, other Black gods.

Dharmakara

DAIKOKU, THE BLACK GOD OF RICHES

W. Crooke reports: "Among other black gods may be named the Japanese Dai Gaku, "the great black one," who is a god of riches."[64] Dai Gaku (also known as Daikoku) is the Japanese god of wealth and good fortune. He is one of the "Seven Lucky Gods," or Kami, of Shintoism, the ancient religion of Japan.

He was probably based on the Hindu god of battle, Mahākāla (*maha* means great, and *kala* means black). Mahākāla was a Black warrior sometimes portrayed as an attendant of the high god Shiva, but sometimes as another personality of Shiva himself.

As an attendant of Shiva, he is often represented outside the main doorway of early North Indian temples. As Shiva himself, his blackness represents both the absorption

Daikoku

and absence of all colors, so he signifies the ultimate or absolute reality. This principle is known in Sanskrit as "*nirguna*," or "being beyond all quality and form."[65]

Mahākāla is a *Dharmapala* ("protector of dharma") in Vajrayana Buddhism, and a deity in Chinese and Japanese Buddhism. He is known as Daheitian (大黑天) in Chinese, and Daikoku-ten (大黒天) in Japanese. Both names translate to "Great Black God." Mahākāla started out as a Black warrior, but was soon associated with good fortune and farming.

According to the *Soka Gakkai Dictionary of Buddhism:*

> The Japanese name Daikoku-ten means the Great Black God, and he was usually painted as a black figure with a furious expression. Iching (635-713) says in The Record of Southern Countries, a record of his travels in India, that an image of Mahakala was installed in the kitchens of the temples in India, and that it carried a bag of gold in its hand, indicating the power to bestow good fortune. Daikoku was introduced in this form to China and Japan, where he became an object of popular belief, evolving from a kitchen deity to the god of rice and rice fields. In the Edo period (1600-1867) in Japan, Daikoku was depicted in painting and sculpture with a happy expression and widely worshiped, together with Ebisu, who is also a god of wealth and one of the seven beneficent deities.[66]

Painting of Bishamon - Hidden Library Cave, Dunhuang, China

In other words, Daikoku was once a fierce Black warrior god, sometimes associated with farming and the success of one's rice crops. By the 17th century, Daikoku was widely known as the happy-looking, pudgy, "good luck" god of farmers, food, and good fortune.

BISHAMON, THE BLACK WARRIOR

Bishamon is another one of the seven good Kami. His name means "the Black Warrior." Bishamon (sometimes known as Bishamonten or Tamonten) is one of the guardian kings of the four quarters. The color black is also associated with the Northern quarter of the compass in which he watches over.

Statue of Bishamon

In China and Japan, he is considered the "Buddhacized" version of the black-skinned Hindu god Kubera. The latter is worshipped in India as the lord of the north, wealth, and treasure, and his name is rendered variously as Kuvera, Jambhāla, and Vaiśravana, as he was said to be the son of the Indian sage Vishrava.

As one of "Japan's Seven Lucky Gods," he often appears friendly and jolly (as do all members of the seven), but he was originally the Hindu god of wealth and buried treasure. Kubera is sometimes considered the king of the Yaksha, powerful earth deities who guard the world's wealth, such as gold and silver.

FUDO MYO-O, THE SUPREME GUARDIAN

Fudō Myō-ō is one of the most popular deities of Japan, and the most commonly depicted of the heavenly kings. Fudō Myō-ō, whose name means "Immovable," is considered the "supreme barrier against evil and a subduer of forces hostile to Buddhist Law."

Fudo-Myo-o

According to the *Handbook of Japanese Mythology*:

Fudō is portrayed carrying a sword and a rope to bind evildoers. His body is usually black or blue. His eyes are staring, and his facial expression is fierce…Fudō stands or sits cross-legged on a rock, signifying his immobility and steadfastness, and is surrounded by flames.[67]

This character may have been imported from India, where he would have arrived after originally being worshipped in the Near East/Caucasus area. We'll explain the background to this theory in Volume Four of *The Science of Self*.

THE KAMUI OF THE AINU

The Ainu are the indigenous people of Japan. They look like they were once related to the aboriginal people of Australia, but these groups have long been separated. In *When the World was Black*, you can see how these people were once dark-skinned and frizzy haired with strong Australoid features, but nowadays these features are muted.

These people first settled Japan tens of thousands of years ago. Their religious traditions have surprisingly remained quite stable, and are a lot like other communities who have been around for more than 10,000 years. That is, they use mythology to describe the elements of nature (which indigenous people often understand very accurately), but don't have many "personal gods." The elemental forces of the Ainu are known as *kamui*. Tōkyō Daigaku has written:

> The category of supernatural beings that received the greatest emphasis among the Ainu is the kamui. Except for the Ainu culture-hero, Aeoina Kamui, all kamui are spirits of natural phenomena. In the supernatural world **kamui take the form of Ainus**. They have families, settlements, and even headmen. They may visit the land of the Ainu.[68]

AE-OINA KAMUI, THE TEACHER

For the most part, these kamui were understood to represent natural forces. That is, as noted in the quote above, with the exception of the "teacher god" Ae-oina Kamui, who is regarded as the founder of Ainu culture. He is the one who came among the Ainu to teach them their arts, from agriculture to ceramics to home-building.

What did he look like? Unfortunately, the Ainu – like most other indigenous people of similar age – typically didn't make representative art. Like the Andaman Islanders and the Australian Aborigines, most of their art was figurative and abstract – that is, geometric designs and carvings.

But there might be a clue in the god's name. The lone "human" god of the Ainu was also known as Ainu-rak-kur and Okikurumi. In Ainu and in Japanese, the words *kur* and *kuru* mean "dark" or "black."[69] Black is found in both names. The more popular name of the two, Ainu-rak-kur, is especially notable, because it roughly translates to "Black Man God."

BLACK DEMONS?

Across rural communities in Japan, there are legends describing "Black demons" inhabiting the hillsides and mountains where the Ainu and other indigenous populations once lived. Although later populations came to fear these beings, such as the *tengu*, it's likely that these myths were originally based on native Black populations. They may

Tengu Mask, 1450 AD

actually refer to the "little Black people" who came to Japan even before the Ainu. Such people had been forced into isolation in these areas when foreign populations took over. If and when people saw Black people leaving the mountainsides, they must have been frightened, having never seen Black-skinned people before.

Do these myths have anything in common with the legends associated with the little Black people of China, like Mo-lê? What about the myths we discuss in northern Europe?

THE PACIFIC ISLANDS

As far east as the Pacific Islands, there are legendary Black deities. Many are hard to trace today, but some, like Degei, are exceptional examples of historical Black leaders being transformed into Gods.

DEGEI, THE AFRICAN KING OF FIJI

Fiji is an island nation in the South Pacific, comprising over 300 islands. Its largest island is Viti Levu (or "Great Fiji"), where most Fijians live today. There, *Degei* is widely known as the Supreme God of the indigenous people.

Degei (or Ndengei) is a Black god who shares traits with many others. He is said to have hatched from an egg, from which the first humans came to Earth. He was once more involved in human affairs, but he withdrew to live (sometimes as a snake) in a cave near the peak of the mountain Uluda. From there, he sometimes causes earthquakes and floods if the people incur his wrath.

Degei is not simply regarded as a black-skinned deity, but he is widely known to be based on the legend of an actual African leader. According to the oral tradition of the indigenous people of Fiji, a legendary warrior chief named Lutanasobasoba led his people to Fiji from somewhere across the seas.

From where did they come? One textbook on Fiji reports, "Most authorities agree that people came into the Pacific from East Africa or South East Asia via Indonesia."[70] The oral tradition is more specific. The Fijians say Chief Lutanasobasoba sailed from Lake Tanganyika in East Africa. They eventually arrived in Fiji on the west coast of Viti Levu, the chief was immortalized as Degei, and his people moved inland into the mountains.

Today, the Fijian government recognizes this origin story as historical fact, and most Fijians trace themselves back to their African ancestor Lutanasobasoba.[71]

THE WORLD WAS BLACK *

How come you're more likely to find people portraying their devils with Black skin than to find people doing the same with their gods? This might be what you'll find in many parts of the world nowadays, but it wasn't always this way. It's just the way things changed when the world's power structure changed. There was a time when our ancestors revered and respected dark skin. In many places, even as far removed from Africa as 16th century China – indigenous people glamorized darkness.

In their masterful summary of early European accounts of their travels in Asia, Lach and Van Kley report that "Asians were variously described as brown, yellow, yellow-brown, black-brown, and coal black or pitch black," and that despite the lighter complexions of many East Asians, "most Asians did not admire white skin, occasionally comparing it to lepers' skin.[72]

Thus it is no surprise that Italian explorer Marco Polo reported that the people he visited in India were in love with their Blackness:

> The darkest man is here the most highly esteemed and considered better than the others who are not so dark. Let me add that in very truth these people portray and **depict their gods and their idols black and their devils white as snow. For they say that God and all the saints are black and the devils are all white**. That is why they portray them as I have described.

So what happened? The world changed! As I explain in *When the World was Black,* the world was first settled by Black people who began leaving East Africa over 100,000 years ago. These people ultimately settled the entire planet.

And the evidence suggests that most of these people remained Black well into the past 10,000 years. In other words, most of the last several million years of human history were "Black history." This is ironic when you consider how Black history is taught in most schools nowadays. By the time we start seeing ancient civilizations with deities of great significance, the world was still predominantly dark-skinned. Thus, whether we find that a deity was based on a historical personality or some positive force based on abstract ideas, this deity was very likely to be portrayed as dark-skinned. Only later did these Black gods become transformed into white gods, Black demons, or colorless abstractions.

---

* An excerpt from the follow up to this book, tentatively titled *The Origins of Religion.*

THE GODS OF THE NEAR EAST

FROM ANU TO ZOROASTER

"God was manifested in the flesh, justified in the spirit, seen by the angels." – Timothy 3:16

In this section, we'll talk about the gods of the ancient Near East. We'll explore the gods of Judaism, Christianity, Islam, Zoroastrianism, and other ancient religions from the region. What you'll learn is that many of these deities weren't abstract, invisible forces, but Black gods of flesh and blood.

THE GOD(S) OF JUDAISM

I'll tell you something that might bother you. Despite the Christian Church's attempt to hold a monopoly on monotheism, the Old Testament doesn't actually teach that there's only one God. Seriously.

Even the commandment that "Thou shalt not keep other gods" doesn't dictate that other gods don't exist. The commandment was simply a demand that this one God was the boss of them all, and would accept no competition for attention from those who would follow this tradition.

So, no, not as "monotheistic" as some may think. In fact, there are several different gods identified in the books of the Old Testament, with names like El, Elohim, YHWH, Baal, Adonai, Yah, Shaddai, and so on. This is because the Old Testament is a compilation of many different traditions from all over the Near East.

This is a difficult concept for people who don't actually read the Bible. If you take the time to simply read the Book of Genesis, however, you'll see that there are two divergent traditions in the very beginning of this book! The first chapter of Genesis describes the creation process one way, and the story is told differently in the second chapter. If you were to look up the original documents, you'd also learn that each tradition refers to a God of a different name.

Again, you don't have to take my word for it. You simply have to read the Bible and see for yourself. This is well-known among Biblical scholars, who have identified at least four separate source documents for the Book of Genesis alone. But, of course, it's not widely taught in the Church, where these ideas might cause people to lose their faith. I'll assume you're more open-minded than that, and I won't waste any more time attempting to make things sound smooth to spare people's feelings.

WHY DIFFERENT TRADITIONS IN ONE RELIGION?

Why do we find different traditions in a book that most people believe is the unadulterated word of God? Because, as we've noted about the religions of India, China, Egypt, and pretty much anywhere else thousands of people lived in distinct communities, different groups of people will develop different traditions. They'll come up with different gods, different heroes, and different founders. I'm sure there was some sort of "root tradition" way back in the distant past, but some of these Gods aren't just going by different names. They came from very different communities, and may have once referred to different people. Yes, people.

El, God of the Bible

Throughout the Old Testament, God is often described as the spirit or consciousness that transcends all space and time, having made the universe which he later chose to call home. More often, however, God is described in very human language. He makes mistakes, he gets angry, he changes his mind, he gets jealous, all kinds of very human stuff. In the Book of Exodus, Moses is able to not only speak to God "face to face, as a man speaks to his friend," but he later convinces God to change his mind.

THE ANTHROPOMORPHIC GOD

In Genesis, Adam and Eve are hiding from God in the Garden of Eden, and God can't find them. They hear his footsteps when he approaches their hiding place. Again, very human stuff. The authors of these scriptures recorded dozens of instances where God is described either as a man (Genesis 2:8, 18:1-3, Exodus 15:3, 24:9-11, 33:11, etc.), as Black (Daniel 7:9), or as a group of men (Genesis 3:22, 11:7).

It's clear that these writers thought of their God as "anthropomorphic," meaning they saw him as flesh and blood, only surpassing them in knowledge and power. At the same time, man himself is often described as possessing the spirit and agency of the Creator, having the potential to become Gods, and being God by nature (Psalms 82:6). The anthropomorphic (human) nature of God goes hand-in-hand with man's potential for *theosis* (becoming God). Knowing this helps us understand the teachings of the Hebrew community in better context.

Statue of El, God of the Bible

EL AND ELOHIM

One of the words used for God in the Old Testament is Elohim, which actually means "Gods" in Hebrew. Elohim is the plural of El, a popular name for the God of the Old Testament. El (or Eloh), is merely a botched transliteration of the original Hebrew name. The vowel points were added later, changing the "A" (or Aleph) to "E" and thus turning Al (or Allah?) into El or Eloh.

This was the work of the Jewish Masoretic scribes who were given the task of rewriting (and editing) the Old Testament by hand around the 6th century AD. This isn't a "secret" by the way. Several texts on the history of the Bible have addressed its many revisions. And the god El, by whatever name you call him, was definitely first regarded as a man, as can be seen in early Canaanite figurine where El is sculpted from gold, but his hands and face are dark.

The word Elohim (or Allahim), is also used to refer to the group of men who were regarded as the leaders of the Hebrew people, the Judges.

YHWH, THE UNSPEAKABLE REALITY

Another popular term for God in the Old Testament is YHWH. YHWH is not meant to be pronounced as "Jehovah." Nor should it be pronounced Yahweh. These four letters, known as the *Tetragrammaton* (which literally means "four letters") are referred to as the "Ineffable Name" which means it could not be said. Even today, orthodox Jews refuse to utter this name or write it.

But why? This unspeakable name contains a secret. The Hebrew letters of YHWH, when from top to bottom, represents the form of a man. This is why the name was left unsaid. It's because these letters don't represent a phonetic word, but pictorially represent the reality of God, like a hieroglyphic.

And these letters do not simply the secret that God was a man, but that he was a Black man. These secrets are the subject of Judaism's esoteric (or hidden) tradition, which we know as the Kabbalah. In *The Doctrine and Literature of the Kabalah*, Arthur Edward Waite writes:

> As it is to the Lesser Countenance that the name of Tetragrammaton is attributed, it follows that the secret of the Zohar is the mystic utterance of the adept to the recipiendary of the Egyptian mysteries: "Osiris is a black god." Microprosopus is, however, "neither the Ahriman of the Persians nor the evil principle of the Manichaeans, but a more exalted concept, a mediating shadow between the infinite light and the feeble eyes of humanity; a veil made in the likeness of humanity with which God Himself deigns to cover His glory; a shadow which contains the reason of all mysteries, explaining the terrible Deity of the prophets, who threatens and inspires fear.

In other words, the secret of the Kabbalah is that the "immanent

God" – the one who appears on Earth (called the "Lesser Countenance") – is a Black god.

This god, Waite writes, is not evil, but a "more exalted concept." His blackness is the skin which God wraps himself in. It is a "veil made in the likeness of humanity with which God Himself deigns to cover His glory." The blackness of his appearance not only "contains the reason of all mysteries," but also "threatens and inspires fear" in all those who do not understand why God would be so Black.

This brings us to the question of how the Black God became associated with Satan.

HOW SATAN BECAME BLACK

In an 1867 essay titled "Satan, The Black-Skinned Man," Ernst Christian L. von Bunsen writes about Job and the Hebrews' sojourn through the Near East. It is on this journey that they encounter "adversaries" who Bunsen said represented the Devil himself:

> Job and his friends were exposed, as much as the Hebrews inhabiting Arabia, to the depredations of other nomadic tribes…Of some of his adversaries Job said, that their fathers he would have 'disdained to have set with the dogs' of his flock. They were thin from 'want and hunger;' they 'gnawed the wilderness, the old desert and desolation;' they 'cut up mallows by the bushes, and juniper roots for their meat; they were driven forth from among men, they cried after them as after a thief; in deserted valleys they must dwell, in holes of the earth and in rocks; among the bushes they roar; under the nettles they were gathered together, children of godless, yea of base men, expelled from the earth.'

WHO WERE THESE SAVAGES?

In this passage, Job is referring to the *troglodytes*, or cave-dwellers, who inhabited the caverns and mountains of the ancient Near East and Caucasus. We know these were the ancestors of Indo-European people, yet Von Bunsen assumes they must have been Black. He continues:

> In the time of Job, as in the time of Abraham, the adversary was Ham. The Hamites, the godless men, not only interfered with their property, but also with their faith. For, in the days of Job, ' the sons of God came to stand before the Lord, and the adversary (the Satan) came also to stand before the Lord.
>
> And the Lord said unto the adversary: From whence comest thou? And the adversary answered the Lord and said: From going to and fro on the earth, and from walking up and down on the same.' This

is what the Hamites had done, who were gradually conquered on the Indus, and returned to the West under Aryan rule. They had gone to and fro, from West to East, and from East to West.

In other words, Bunsen is using Biblical scripture to argue that Ham was the great adversary, simply because the Hamites traveled the world and built civilizations everywhere. The connecting being made here was that Satan, the "adversary," was a Black man.

THE BLACK MAN IS THE DEVIL?

Von Bunsen is suggesting that the Black man is the devil. He's not only talking about Ham himself as the "adversary," but all of the Hamites (Black people). Of course, he's basing this on the false premise that Job's enemies were Black (when they were actually white), but this idea found a welcome home in the minds of many Christians of the time. Von Bunsen continues to explain:

Whilst the men of Japhet, the Aryans, were exclusively of 'high degree,' and the men of Ham, the non-Aryans, exclusively of low degree, the upper castes of the men of Shem were, as we tried to explain, of white descent, and the lower castes of dark descent...

What had been accomplished on the Indus, and in other Eastern districts, that is, the subjugation of non-Aryan, black, or Hamitic races, was to be done between the Nile and the Euphrates.

Aryan Shepherd Kings had established their rule in Egypt, but 'the black-skinned man,' the Kedur, or Kedar, later called 'Mapula,' or 'the ravager of the West,' was the great 'adversary' of the Aryans in the land of Kenaan.

He and his black host were 'base' men, 'men of low degree,' and 'godless men,' who opposed ' the sons of God,' and claimed the privilege of ministering unto the same God in the same sanctuary...

[B]oth the Aryan and his non-Aryan adversary, or Satan, strove, in the time of Job, as in the time of Abraham, for supremacy in these favoured lands.[73]

In other words, the fact that Black people were conquered by whites across the ancient world, and that these whites were competing for "supremacy in these favored lands"…somehow tells Von Bunsen (and others who agreed with him) that Black people were no different from another great adversary, the Devil.

This is just one of many examples of how ancient traditions could be rewritten or reinterpreted to echo the prevailing racial sentiments of the time. There exists nothing in the original scriptures to suggest that Job's "adversaries" were Hamites. Yet through a stretch of logic and language, Von Bunsen has made it seem as if this was the case.

IS WHITE THE COLOR OF GOOD?

Other factors helped promote the idea that the Devil was indeed Black. For example, the Christian world adopted much of its iconic imagery of what the Devil looked like from the African god Bes, who we discuss elsewhere in this book.

> *"There is no other Devil but God himself painted black."* – H.P. Blavatsky, 1894

Most importantly, however, those who wrote these books argued that white was the color of good, and that white men were inherently good, arguing the opposite about the color black and those who have black skin. Such arguments became especially popular among those who hoped to justify Christian slavery.

To this point, it seems especially ironic that those who sought to justify the world's greatest inhumanities felt it reasonable to cast their victims as devils and the perpetrators as the children of God. In 1894, H.P. Blavatsky, founder of the esoteric Theosophical Society, asserted:

> The devil is the Middle Ages with their phantoms and stakes.
> The devil is the Inquisition, torturing genius and gagging science.
> The devil is Alexander VI burning Savonarola at the stake.
> *Osiris is a black god.*
> The devil of god is the god of the devil.[74]

It took me a few minutes to process what was being said here, but it struck a chord when it hit me. I don't agree with everything Blavatsky promoted, but this passage speaks volumes, at least for those who understand.

Unfortunately, when it comes to concepts like these, not many will understand. Even with the secret traditions where European initiates learn that "Osiris is a Black God," outsiders came to associate these traditions with the worship of Satan, who they thought of as the only "dark god." This is, in fact, how so many secret societies became associated with Satanism, when they had originally been studying the secret that God was a Black man.

IRAN AND THE CAUCASUS

Through the work of Von Bunsen and others like him, it was easy to firmly establish the idea that Satan was a Black-skinned man in the minds of the Christian world. Thousands of years ago, a similar switch was conducted in the Near East. This is the story of how Black gods in Iran and the Caucasus came to be associated with evil.

The Gods of Zoroastrianism

Ahura Mazda

In many parts of the world, particularly those where there was a racial conflict between Blacks and whites, we find that Black gods have become known as devils, while the forces of evil – who were once represented as white – have now become known as Gods. This is the case in India, Sri Lanka, the Caucasus, and Iran, as well as other areas, though to a lesser extent.

The older the reversal, the more widespread the new belief. Thus, in parts of South Africa and Australia where Westerners have attempted to vilify native Black gods and replace them with white Gods within the past hundred years or so, such ideas aren't as widely accepted as they are in places where the idea was introduced a few thousand years ago.

This is the case with the two deities of Zoroastrianism. Zorastrianism isn't well-known nowadays (although it is still practiced by many Iranians), but beginning sometime around 1,000 B.C., it was the predominant religion of the Near East, specifically around modern-day Iran and the Caucasus Mountains.

Its founder, Zoroaster (sometimes Zarathustra) taught of two gods who were in constant competition. It may have been one of the first religions to promote a serious duality between good and evil, personified by the gods Ahura Mazda and Angro-Mainyus. Today, these names are typically translated as something like "Illuminating Wisdom" and "Destructive Spirit."

Angro-Mainyus, the Black Mind

According to historian George Rawlinson, the name "Ahura Mazda" means either "the much-knowing spirit," the "much-giving spirit," the "all-bountiful," or "the all-wise." Conversely, Rawlinson says, the name of Angro-Mainyus signified that he was black:

> "Angro" is akin to "niger," and so to "negro;" it means simply "black" or "dark." "Mainyus," a substantive, is the exact equivalent of the Latin "mens," and the Greek ixtvos. It means "mind,"

"intelligence." Thus Angro-Mainyus is the "black or dark intelligence."

We also know, linguistically speaking, that "man" means "mind," so Angro-Mainyus could also mean "Black man." What we know for sure is that these two were in "perpetual warfare" from the beginning. Rawlinson explains:

> Whatever good thing Ahura-Mazda had created, Angro-Mainyus had corrupted and ruined it. Moral and physical evils were alike at his disposal. He could blast the earth with barrenness, or make it produce, thorns, thistles, and poisonous plants; his were the earthquake, the storm, the plague of hail, the thunderbolt; he could cause disease and death, sweep off a nation's flocks and herds, by murrain, or depopulate a continent by pestilence; ferocious wild beasts, serpents, toads, mice, hornets, mosquitoes, were his creation; he had invented and introduced into the world the sins of witchcraft, murder, unbelief, cannibalism; he excited wars and tumults, continually stirred up the bad against the good, and labored by every possible expedient to make vice triumph over virtue, Ahura-Mazda could exercise no control over him; the utmost that he could do was to keep a perpetual watch upon his rival, and seek to, baffle and defeat him. This he was, not always able to do; despite his best endeavors, Angro-Mainyus was [often] victorious.[75]

This sounds pretty bad for Angro-Mainyus, the "Black man" of Zoroastrianism. However, you have to understand the history of the region that produced this tradition. As we'll explain in Volume Four of the *Science of Self* series, this area was where the conflict between Black and white really took shape. The battles between these two gods were symbolic of the perpetual warfare between Blacks and whites in this area.

The whites who came to dominate Iran were eventually able to turn Angro-Mainyus into a bad guy, but he may have simply symbolized the Blacks who kept repelling their ancestors back into the "barren" Caucasus. This is where they encountered all the evils Rawlinson describes above.

CZERNY-BOG

For the same reason, the Slavonic myths of southeastern Europe describe a "Black god" known as Czerny-Bog. According to Gerald Massey, "Czerny-Bog was also the dark Deity of the Anglo-Saxons called Zernebok." Both Slavonic and Anglo-Saxon people considered this god to be evil, but only because he forced their ancestors to live in this awful "land of darkness" and killed them when they attempted to leave. There are also Caucasian myths known as the

Nart Sagas that tell the same story, describing the Black warriors who "escorted" them into the Caucasus thousands of years ago.[76]

According to *Merriam-Webster's Encyclopedia of World Religions*:

Common to Slavic Eurasia is a deity called Zcerneboch (or Chernobog), the Black God, and Tiarnoglofi, the Black Head (Mind or Brain). The Black God survives in numerous Slavic curses, and the aid of the White God is sought to obtain protection or mercy in Bulgaria, Serbia, and Pomerania. This religious dualism of white and black gods is common to practically all the peoples of Eurasia.[77]

Throughout this book, you'll see other examples of Black gods who were transformed into devils and demons across Eurasia. In most cases, these gods were based on historical warriors, guards, sentinels, and other military figures who – in ancient times – may have been a source of fear and hostility for early Caucasians.

MESOPOTAMIAN RELIGION

Long before the Bible described Babylon as a place of great evils, ancient Mesopotamia (modern-day Iraq) was home to many thriving Black civilizations. Skipping over the long history of this region (You can see *When the World was Black, Part Two* for this), we can jump right into the gods and goddesses of these civilizations.

ANU, ISHTAR, AND ENLIL

In 1915, W.E.B. Du Bois discussed the Black people of ancient Mesopotamia in his

Statue of Enlil

work *The Negro*:

> That Negro peoples were the beginners of civilization along the Ganges, the Euphrates, and the Nile seems proven. Early Babylon was founded by a Negroid race. Hammurabi's code, the most ancient known, says "Anna [Anu] and Bel [Baal] called me, Hammurabi the exalted prince, the worshiper of the gods; to cause justice to prevail in the land, to destroy the wicked, to prevent the strong from oppressing the weak, to go forth like the sun over the black-head race, to enlighten the land, and to further the welfare of the people."[79]

A passage from the renowned Babylonian *Epic of Gilgamesh* says something similar about Enlil, the son of Anu:

> Father Enlil, Lord of the countries,
>
> Father Enlil, Lord of the True Word,
>
> Father Enlil, Pastor of the Blacks...

Anu was the high god of the ancient Sumerians, sometimes describes as a "sky god." Anu was considered the god of heaven, the lord of constellations, and the king of gods, spirits and demons, dwelling in the highest heavenly regions. But Anu may have not represented an invisible concept at first. Instead, he may have been based on an actual group of people known as the Anu, who left Nubia to found the ancient civilizations of Egypt and Mesopotamia.

In *The African Origin of Civilization*, Cheikh Anta Diop notes:

> In this epic, Anu, the primitive god, father of Ishtar, has the same Negro name as Osids the Onian. "The goddess Ishtar took the floor and spoke thus the god Anu her father..." We have already seen that, according to Amelineau, the Anu were the first Blacks to inhabit Egypt. A number of them remained in Arabia Petraea throughout Egyptian history. The Negro Anu is thus an historical fact, not a mental concept or a working hypothesis.

In *Great African Thinkers*, Runoko Rashidi corroborates Diop's claims:

> Anu was the great father of the gods, including Ishtar and Enlil, in Sumerian religious mythology. Anu was also a name frequently associated with the early Blacks of the Nile Valley and related areas. The Anu Seti, for example, lived on the banks of the Upper Nile, in the Sudan. The Anu-Tehennu were the early Black inhabitants of Libya.

In his *Religions of the Ancient World*, historian George Rawlinson quotes Babylonian traditions describing the god Anu:

> Anu is commonly spoken of as "the old Anu," "the original chief," "the king of the lower world," and "the lord of spirits and demons"...He [Anu] constructed dwellings for the great gods; he fixed the constellations, whose figures were like animals. He made the year into portions; he divided it; twelve months he established,

with their constellations, three by three. And from among the days of the year he appointed festivals; he made dwellings for the planets, for their rising and for their setting.

This all makes sense when we refer back to Diop, who says:

These Blacks [the Anu] were probably the first to practice agriculture, to irrigate the valley of the Nile, build dams, invent sciences [particularly astronomy], arts, writing, the calendar. They created the cosmogony contained in *The Book of The Dead*, texts which leave no doubt about the Negroness of the race that conceived the ideas.

Anu

In other words, great Black people often become worshipped as great Black gods and goddesses.

NIMROD, THE MIGHTY HUNTER

You may recognize the name Nimrod from the Bible as well. Like Babylon, he gets a pretty bad rap. In both cases, this is mostly because of regional competition. The Hebrew authors of the Old Testament simply couldn't cosign the traditions of Babylon, because they intended to replace those traditions with their own. That's why they considered Baal (a "good" Babylonian god) a "false idol," yet adopted the Canaanite El as one of their own.

So who was Nimrod? As king of Shinar, he was considered the founder of Babylon and a man of great power. In Genesis 10:8-9, he is described as a "mighty hunter before the Lord." In 1852, Biblical historian Josiah Priest wrote that Nimrod, like the Greek Hercules (who we'll discuss in another chapter), was originally a Black man who later became revered as a Black god:

Canaanite figure of El

As to Nimrod, the hero of Babel, being the great type of all the Herculeses of the ancient nations, there can be no doubt; for the legends of every country who have claimed him to be a god, represent him as always being armed with a club of enormous size, with which he slew the monsters of the earth — dreadful serpents, wild beasts, &c.

In this very character the Bible represents him; see Gen. x, 8, 9, where it is written, that he was a mighty hunter, before the Lord, which the Jewish rabbis interpret of his slaying wild beasts, which at that time greatly infested the country of the Euphrates, where he lived before he and Cush, his father, and Ham, his grandfather, went to Africa and founded Ethiopia...Nimrod, the grandson of Ham, was a negro, and after his death became a negro god by deification, after the manner of the ancients...[80]

Priest adds that the Greek myths of Hercules may have been derived from the Black Babylonian, Nimrod.

ISLAM AND ARABIA

Islam is one of the world's largest religions, with over a billion adherents across the world. In the year 610, the Prophet Muhammad began preaching faith in Mecca that would soon sweep across the Middle East, and – before long – the rest of the world.

Islam was, indeed, a monotheistic religion, because – unlike the other two Abrahamic religions, Judaism or Christianity – Prophet Muhammad was adamant that "There is no God but Allah." Allah, the one God of the Muslim world, is almost never described in anthropomorphic language. There are some exceptions to that rule, however.

Allah and Adam

The Islamic world has many sects and traditions, but most Muslims today think of God as entirely spirit, having no parts or partnerships, and being impossible to comprehend with the physical eye. Yet this may not have always been the case. In *Knowledge of Self*, we write:

> In the Qur'an, Allah is described as having a face that believers will see in the last days (presumably after death). The Qur'an makes mentions of Allah's "hands" being tied down, but otherwise, the Neo-Platonic influence on Islam is strong. Still, Allah makes Adam out of Black mud to be His Khalifa, or vicegerent, on Earth. A vicegerent is a successor responsible for handling the duties of his predecessor.

We could interpret these facts as suggestion that Adam, the original man, was the successor of Allah, acting as a god on Earth. Most Islamic scholars, however, are adamant that Adam was nothing more than man, and that Allah has never been regarded as anything other than spirit. Few scholars have attempted to argue anything different, despite the fact that many early schools of Islamic thought, like that of Ibn Hanbal, advocated otherwise.

In recent years, this topic has been thoroughly addressed by Dr. Wesley Muhammad, who completed his doctoral dissertation on the subject, titled *Tajalli Wa-Ru'ya: A Study of Anthropomorphic Theophany and Visio Dei in the Hebrew Bible, the Qur'an and Early Sunni Islam*. Several of Dr. Muhammad's other published works go into considerable depth on whether Allah was ever regarded as a man, and whether he was, in fact, regarded as a Black man.

To make sense of this subject, we need to place the origins of Islamic theology in historical context, by looking at what the people of Arabia believed about Allah before Prophet Muhammad came.

AL-UZZAH, ALLAT, AND MANAH

Islam is one of the few world religions that is strongly monotheistic, in a way that neither Judaism or Christianity can claim. Yet, before the Prophet Muhammad began tearing down the hundreds of "idols" found in Mecca, Allah was not alone. In his *Book of God*, Dr. Wesley Muhammad explains:

> Al-Uzza, along with Allat and Manah, were three pagan goddesses considered to be the "Daughters of Allah" to the pagan Arabs. At the time of Muhammad, Al-Uzzah received the most worship. Her shrine was located in Nakhla, a few miles north of Mecca. In the eighth year after the Hegira (Muhammad's flight from Mecca to Medina), Muhammad sent the zealous and valiant Khalid with thirty horseman to destroy the sanctuary. While Khalid was putting the sanctuary to the sword, a naked black woman "with flowing hair" approached him. The lady's priest, who was also present, cried out: "Be courageous, AI 'Uzza, and protect yourself!" K.halid, it is written, "shook with terror." After regaining his composure and courage, he cleft the Black woman's head and killed her. Khalid reported the deed to Muhammad, expressing doubt that he had actually slain Al-Uzzah herself. He suggested that the Black Woman was just a priestess.
>
> The Prophet replied, however, "Of a truth, it was Uzza herself whom thou hast destroyed."
>
> This is extremely significant. If the Prophet and the Arabs in general accepted Al-Uzzah as a Black Woman, and the Arabs saw Al-'Uzzah as the "Daughter of Allah," how do you suppose they saw the Father? Though Muhammad and the Holy Qur'an condemns the Arabs' belief that these goddesses are Allah's daughters, they both fail to condemn the anthropomorphism implied. In fact, though Al-Uzzah is not a "Daughter of Allah" in the sense the Arabs believed, the name is the feminine of Al-Aziz, which is one of the 99 Names of Allah.[81]

In *God's Black Prophets*, Dr. Muhammad also makes the case that Prophet Muhammad himself was a Black man.

ALMAQAH, SUPREME BLACK GOD

There's much more to the story of what the people of Arabia believed before Prophet Muhammad came. In Julian Baldick's 1998 work *Black God: The Afroasiatic Roots of the Jewish, Christian, and Muslim Religions*, we learn that – thousands of years before Prophet Mohammed – the original people of Arabia revered a supreme God named *Almaqah*. This deity became the prototype for many of the later "high gods" of the ancient world, and quite possibly even the god of Mohammedan Islam himself. As the title of Baldick's book suggests, Almaqah was a Black god.

Yet throughout this entire book, Baldick never once connects "Black" and "race," choosing, instead, to make the god of the Afro-Asiatic people "black" because he represents a storm cloud! But are all storm clouds pitch black? Did our ancestors truly not understand the weather cycle? And did it make sense to worship a black cloud at a time when ancient Arabia had not yet become a desert (meaning it was not affected by the kind of drought that makes a rainstorm seem like a godsend)?

As to why nobody seriously questioned Baldick's conclusions, I can't imagine. The worst part is this: Almaqah doesn't represent a storm cloud to begin with. Recent studies have concluded that *Almaqah* was a solar deity (or "Sun God") like Egypt's Ra. So why was Almaqah black? Well, why else?

CONCEPTIONS OF CHRIST

"What shall I say of the black Christ among the white Italians, Swiss, Germans, and French? Is it necessary to say anything? Does it not speak for itself?" – Godfrey Higgins, Anacalypsis

Who was Jesus Christ? For centuries after the time of his death, Christian communities debated the specifics of his life and nature. Was he the Son of God, the Son of Man, or both? Did he say and do everything attributed to him in the books of the Bible? Where did he come from, and what did he look like? How much of his story is myth and how much is history? In this section, we'll explore some of the mythology associated with Jesus Christ and the race of the historical Christ.

THE MYTHICAL CHRIST

"It has served us well, this myth of Christ." – Pope Leo X

In *The Five Gospels: What Did Jesus Really Say?*, seventy-seven Biblical scholars argue that, while there was most likely a historical person who we have come to know as Jesus Christ, over 80% of the words attributes to him were not his, but were developed by later writers. This makes sense, considering that most of the writers of the New Testament had never met Jesus, and some weren't even born until long after his death. In fact, Paul, who wrote the majority of the New Testament (authoring at least 13 of the 27 books), had never actually met Jesus, and only claimed to have seen him in a vision.

This is what led Dr. Martin Luther King, Jr. to question the historical background of the Christ myth. While Dr. King appreciated the Christian Church and its Gospel as an effective platform to promote an agenda of social change, he remained a critical thinker. In a research paper titled "A Study in Mithraism," King wrote that Christianity was originally just another "Mystery Religion":

> It is not at all surprising in view of the wide and growing influence of these religions that when the disciples in Antioch and elsewhere preached a crucified and risen Jesus they should be regarded as the heralds of another Mystery Religion, and that Jesus himself should be taken for the divine Lord of the cult through whose death and resurrection salvation was to be had.

King did not believe that the "risen savior" mythology assigned to Christ was unique. Elsewhere he wrote:

> The birth of Jesus is quite similar to the birth of the sons of Zeus. It was believed in Greek thought that an extraordinary person could only be explained by saying that he had a father who was more than human. It is probable that this Greek idea influenced Christian thought.

This was not, however, a new idea. In *The World's Sixteen Crucified Saviors Before Christ*, originally published in 1875, Kersey Graves illustrates how the mythology associated with Jesus Christ bears striking similarities with dozens of other "savior gods" across the ancient traditions of India, Egypt, Persia, Rome, Greece, Mexico, and Tibet.

CHRIST, A BLACK SAVIOR GOD

In a section of *The World's Sixteen Crucified Saviors Before Christ* that often goes ignored, Kersey Graves added something more that is worthy of our attention:

> Here we will note it as a curious circumstance, that several of the above-named Saviors are represented as being black, Jesus Christ included with this number. There is as much evidence that the Christian Savior was a black man, or at least a dark man, as there is of his being the son of the Virgin Mary, or that he once lived and moved upon the earth. And that evidence is the testimony of his disciples, who had nearly as good an opportunity of knowing what his complexion was as the evangelists, who omit to say anything about it. In the pictures and portraits of Christ by the early Christians, he is uniformly represented as being black. And to make this the more certain, the red tinge is given to the lips; and the only text in the Christian bible quoted by orthodox Christians, as describing his complexion, represents it as being black. Solomon's declaration, "I am black, but comely, O ye daughters of Jerusalem"

(Sol. i. 5), is often cited as referring to Christ. According to the bible itself, then, Jesus Christ was a black man.

Christ and His Disciples - Coptic Museum, Cairo

If you thought *that* was exceptional for a white scholar to say in 1875, take a look at what Graves says *next*:

> Let us suppose that, at some future time, he makes his second advent to the earth, as some Christians anticipate he will do, and that he comes in the character of a sable Messiah, how would he be received by our negro-hating Christians, of sensitive olfactory nerves? Would they worship a negro God? Let us imagine he enters one of our fashionable churches, with his "rough and ready," linsey-woolsey, seamless garment on, made of wild sea-grass, thus

presenting a very forbidding appearance, and what would be the result? Would the sexton show him to a seat? Would he not rather point to the door, and exclaim, "Get out of here; no place here for niggers"? What a ludicrous series of ideas is thus suggested by the thought that Jesus Christ was a "darky."

Black historians did not miss the significance of Graves' suggestion. In his 1939 work, *Ethiopia and the Origin of Civilization*, Black historian John G. Jackson compiled a series of important Black gods across Asia and the Americas. He adds:

Most of these black gods were regarded as crucified saviors who died to save mankind by being nailed to a cross, or tied to a tree with arms outstretched as if on a cross, or slain violently in some other manner. Of these crucified saviors, the most prominent were Osiris and Horus of Egypt, Krishna of India, Mithra of Persia, Quetazlcoatl of Mexico, Adonis of Babylonia and Attis of Phrygia. Nearly all of these slain savior-gods have the following stories related about them: They are born of a virgin, on or near Dec. 25th (Christmas); their births are heralded by a star; they are born either in a cave or stable; they are slain, commonly by crucifixion; they descend into hell, and rise from the dead at the beginning of Spring (Easter), and finally ascend into heaven. The parallels between the legendary lives of these pagan messiahs and the life of Jesus Christ as recorded in the Bible are so similar that progressive Bible scholars now admit that stories of these heathen Christs have been woven into the life-story of Jesus.[82]

These "remarkable parallels" were the subject of Jackson's 1938 booklet, *Christianity Before Christ*.

Self-taught scholar J.A. Rogers dedicated countless hours to investigating the race of Christ and other savior Gods across the world. In 1944, he concluded:

The earliest gods and messiahs on all the continents were black. Research has yielded an impressive amount of material on the subject...The Messiahs, some of whom lived many centuries before Christ, had lives which so closely paralleled that of Christ that it seems most likely that the story of the latter was adapted from them. Moreover, the word Christ comes from the Indian, Krishna or Chrisna, which means "The Black One."[83]

"BLACK IS NOT GOD'S COLOR"

Bishop Henry McNeal Turner wasn't the first Black minister to assert that God was Black, or that a white God was preposterous for Black believers. He may have been the most direct in saying so, but Black men like Prince Hall, David Walker, and Henry Highland Garnett had pushed in similar directions long before him. The more vocal they were, the more opposition they met.

It's perhaps no surprise, then, that we don't know much about anyone who was especially vocal about these things before Turner's time. But we know these ideas were spreading, just by noting how many white people (and some Black people) felt the need to attack this idea.

"I hate the black; black is not God's color; white is God's color," wrote Methodist minister Henry Ward Beecher, long before Turner's statement. Sadly, Bishop Turner had once held Minister Beecher, a Northern abolitionist, in high regard. In 1863, Beecher had written:

> The interval between the destruction and the salvation of the Republic is measured by two steps: one is Emancipation; the other Military Success. The first is taken; the other delays. How is it to be achieved? There is but one answer: by the Negro!

> They (the negroes) are the forlorn hope of the Republic. They are the last safe-keepers of the good cause. We must make alliance with them, or our final success is imperiled.

In other words, Beecher had argued, it would only be through arming Black soldiers that the Union could be saved. "God and the Negro are to save the Republic!" the minister proclaimed. Thousands of Black Christians agreed with his sentiments, with Bishop Turner among them. But when it came to what Minister Beecher though about God and the Negro themselves, his true colors came out.

Thus, it seems especially fitting that in December of 1865, Beecher's wife reported:

> A [white] member of their church…had just returned from the South, and there it was reported that she was seen stealing and carrying away the records of St. Peter's church, and that on her return to New York, thousands of colored people met her on the Battery, and that she made a speech to them, in the course of which she had said that **God was black, that Jesus Christ was a mulatto, that the devil was white, and that she only regretted that she was not born black.**[84]

THE BLACK VIRGIN AND CHILD

What about the mother of Christ? Although most paintings and statues of the Virgin Mary depict her as a white woman, these are recent changes.

On April 21, 1979, the newspaper *The Hour* published an article titled "Poland's Sacred Statue is Black Madonna," describing Pope John Paul II's visit to one of the most sacred images in the Christian world:

The mysterious Black madonna of Czestochow is the most sacred icon in Poland…Art experts believe the madonna was painted between the 6th and 8th centuries and say the style is reminiscent of early Egyptian Christian. Legend, however, says the Madonna was painted by the apostle Luke himself and kept hidden in Jerusalem for 500 years before traveling to Poland by way of Istanbul…

In other words, local traditions suggest that this portrayal of Mary went as far back as the time of the Apostles. In other words, this rendition must be quite authentic. Indeed, the Black image of Mary is much older than the white:

Many of the madonnas painted in the earliest centuries of Christiandom were black, according to historians, and it wasn't until the Renaissance that it became popular to give the mother of Christ the features of a Florentine maiden [a white woman].

In other words, before the mother of Christ was depicted as a white woman, she was depicted as a Black woman. In places where the Black Madonna still survives, she is believed to have incredible powers, and receives more intense worship than any other icon. Needless to say, Pope John Paul II was not the only Pope to worship at the foot of the Black Madonna and her son the Black Christ.

In *Anacalypsis*, Godfrey Higgins writes about where these sacred Black Madonnas can still be found across Europe:

In all the Romish [Catholic] countries of Europe, France, Italy, Germany, etc., the God Christ, as well as his mother, are described in their old pictures and statues to be black. The infant God in the arms of his black mother, his eyes and drapery white, is himself perfectly black…

There is scarcely an old church in Italy where some remains of the worship of the BLACK VIRGIN and BLACK CHILD are not to be met with. Very often the black figures have given way to white ones, and in these cases the black ones, as being held sacred, were put into retired places in the churches, but were not destroyed, but are yet to be found there.

Higgins then lists dozens of cathedrals, chapels, and churches across Europe where such iconic images can still be found.[85] Naturally, some of these paintings and statues have since been hidden away, as they were already being hidden (or "retired") even before Higgins published his book.

However, many can still be seen today. If you're ever in Europe, Wikipedia maintains an updated list of places where these images have survived.[86] These icons are also found across Latin America, for reasons we explain in another part of this book.

DID THE IMAGES CHANGE COLOR?

In the distant past, it was simply taken for granted that these icons were Black. When European colonization began, Western scholars began coming up with outlandish explanations to account for their blackness. As early as 1833, Higgins argued against the idea that these images were only colored black or brown because of "discoloration" or an "artistic convention."

He says these images were meant to depict a very real blackness of skin. To those who argue that some statues were colored brown to look like bronze, he says, "the number that are left with white teeth, etc, let out the secret." In other words, why paint something brown to look like a work of bronze, but leave the eyes and teeth white?

To those who argued that smoke and other factors have discolored the paintings and statues, he says:

When the circumstance has been named to the Romish priests [that Christ was painted Black], they have endeavoured to disguise the fact, by pretending that the child had become black by the smoke of the candles; but it was black where the smoke of a candle never came: and, besides, how came the candles not to blacken the white of the eyes, the teeth, and the shirt, and how came they to redden the lips? The mother is, the author believes, always black, when the child is. Their real blackness is not to be questioned for a moment.[87]

In other words, there's a reason why the skin of these characters was Black, but not their eyes, teeth, or clothing. It wasn't candle smoke, and it wasn't an attempt to imitate bronze. It was because these individuals were meant to look like dark-skinned people. It's sad that Higgins debunked these preposterous arguments over a century ago, yet scholars continue to make the same arguments even today.

So why a Black Madonna and Child? Perhaps there was some ancient tradition, like the Black Isis and child Horus, being revived in Europe under Christian pretences. But these color choices could also have been made simply because early Christians knew and understood that the historical Christ and his mother were quite literally Black people.

THE HISTORICAL CHRIST

We've said quite a bit on the mythical elements of the story of Christ. Was there a historical Jesus? I'd say there had to be. I don't think that so many of his alleged contemporaries would have simply agreed on an imaginary person and then wrote about what he taught them. There was most likely a historical person who inspired all this talk. This person may not have, however, said or done all the things ascribed to him by later writers. He may have been no different than the many Black leaders we simply don't have a ton of books about.

After all, how often do we find records of Fard Muhammad (founder of the Nation of Islam) or Allah the Father (founder of the Nation of Gods and Earths) in our history books today? What about the founders of the BLA or RNA? These were important groups who played significant roles in the very recent struggle for Black liberation in America, but it's not exactly easy to find records of who they were and what they did.

THE NAME OF CHRIST

The further back we go in time, the rarer such records become. It doesn't help that we don't know what Jesus's actual name was. It certainly wasn't Jesus Christ. Christ is a title, something like Messiah. And Jesus is the English version of a name that couldn't have been his. The Hebrew language doesn't even have a "J" sound! His name may have been Yeshuah, Yahoshuah, or something similar. If his father's name was Yosef (Joseph), he may have been known as Yeshuah ben Yosef. Unfortunately, there aren't too many historical records of such a person.

WHAT DID HE LOOK LIKE?

In the book of Revelation, Christ (in his return) is described as having feet like burnished bronze (meaning dark brown) and hair like wool. But what did Jesus look like when he lived in Jerusalem? Most scholars agree that he couldn't have looked like the famous portraits we've all seen.

The most popular picture – the one your grandma probably has hanging up in her living room – was based on a European named Caesar Borgia. Similarly, the images adorning the ceilings of the Sistine Chapel were based on the painter Michelangelo's family. But there's no way these individuals really looked like Italians.

Scholars agree that the historical Christ would have at least been brown-skinned. If we look at the fact that Jesus was "hidden" in Egypt at a time when Egyptians were darker than they are now, we can even assume that he may have been darker than the average Arab or Palestinian today. If we factor in the account of John in the book of Revelation, we could even go so far as to assume that the historical Christ was a dark brown complexion with wooly hair.

And this is the image that we find supported by the earliest historical evidence.

WHAT DID JOSEPHUS SAY?

Outside of the books of the New Testament, there's really only one record of a person fitting the description of the historical Jesus. It comes from Josephus, a Jewish historian born a few years after Jesus's death. There's a lot of controversy about this quote, but according to Biblical scholar Robert Eisler's translation, this is how Jesus was described:

> At that time also there appeared a certain man of magic power...if it be meet to call him a man, [whose name is Jesus], whom [certain] Greeks call a son of [a] God, but his disciples [call] the true prophet...he was a man of simple appearance, mature age, black-skinned (melagchrous), short growth, three cubits tall, hunchbacked, prognathous (lit. 'with a long face' [macroprosopos]), a long nose, eyebrows meeting above the nose...with scanty [curly] hair, but having a line in the middle of the head after the fashion of the Nazaraeans, with an undeveloped beard.[88]

Painting of Christ – 300 AD

THE EARLIEST PORTRAITS

Taking this into consideration, it makes sense that all of the earliest paintings of Jesus portray him in this way, dark-skinned with curly hair.

Painting of Jesus – Rome, 530 AD

Painting from Roman Catacombs – circa 300 AD

Same painting – before bleaching

That's how he looks in "The Healing of the Paralytic," regarded as the oldest known image of Jesus, dating from about 235 AD. That's how he (and the Apostles) look in the paintings in the Roman catacombs (circa 300 AD). That's how he looks in a Roman church fresco dating back to 530 AD. That's how he looks in all the images from the churches of Ethiopia, which are regarded as holding most closely to the original traditions of the early Christians. And this is how he looked in that painting James Evans hung up on the wall on that episode of *Good Times*.

As with the images of his mother Mary, Jesus didn't start becoming white until the artists of Renaissance Europe got a hold of him.

MARY IS MOTHER EARTH?

Mary was not the only sacred female to be depicted as a Black woman. In *The Cult of the Black Virgin*, Ean Begg notes that more than 500 of the world's "Madonna" icons are Black or dark-skinned. Begg connects this tradition to much older "pagan" traditions representing Black female divinities across Europe. In 1900, an author named W. Crooke had come to the same conclusion:

> English tradition supplies us with a black Godiva, who is doubtless a decayed deity of the older paganism. In more modern times we have the host of Black Madonnas, a very curious chapter in the history of hagiology. The legends given in explanation of their colour are of many kinds...Blackness is the characteristic of images other than Madonnas, such as the rag images of the Italian Befanas, which take the place of our Santa Claus and have blackened faces. [89]

In other words, pretty much any important "sacred female" across

Christian Europe was originally Black. As you'll see throughout the book, this is also true in the Near East, Africa, and Asia.

This could have been because of older traditions where the Black woman was revered as a divine figure. For example, many scholars say the worship of the Egyptian Isis could have made its way into Christian Europe at a very early age. Some of the images of the Black Madonna and Child look just like older statues of the Egyptian Isis and child Horus.

Yet these traditions are found far beyond ancient Egypt, and may be thousands of years older. In *Sex and the Garden of Eden Myth*, Maynard Shipley makes this clear:

> Very suggestive is the fact that representations of the virgin mother and infant savior are often black. This is true in the case of the paintings and images of Isis and Horus, of Devaki and Krishna, and in many cases of Mary and Jesus. The most ancient pictures and statues in Italy and other parts of Europe, which are adored by the faithful as representations of the Virgin Mary and the infant Jesus, reveal the infant draped in white, but with face black and in the arms of a black mother....
>
> How does it happen that the Virgin Mother of the Mexican Savior-God so closely resembled the Black Virgins of Egypt and Europe? Had they not all a common origin?[90]

It is possible, then, that both Mary and Isis are local versions of a timeless tradition revering mother Earth itself as a Black woman. According to Stephen Benko, "the Black Madonna is the ancient earth-goddess converted to Christianity." He identifies several Black goddesses, such as Artemis of Ephesus, Isis, Ceres, and others, all of whom are tied to the ideas of agriculture and fertility.

Benko notes the presence of the earth-mother concept in Adam's creation in Genesis 2:7, and sees a parallel to the 'New Creation' in which Christ is the 'New Adam.' He argues that Mary is equivalent to the Earth of the first creation, citing 4th century Archbishop Ambrose who said, "from the virgin earth Adam, Christ from the virgin." Ambrose's pupil, the African church father Saint Augustine, also taught that "the Virgin Mary represents the earth and that Jesus is of the earth born." This was actually once a well-known teaching.

For example, the Maronite Liturgy alludes to Mary being the Earth during the offering of the bread which symbolizes Christ:

> I am the bread of life, said Our Lord.
> From on high I came to earth so all might live in me.
> Pure word without flesh I was sent from the Father.
> Mary's womb received me like good earth [does] a grain of wheat.

Behold, the priest bears me aloft to the altar.

Alleluia. Accept our offering.

Benko, however doesn't believe that Mary's blackness is to be seen literally. According to him, the best fertile soil is black in color and the blacker it is, the better it is for farming. This may be true, but it's not the reason why these sacred mothers were portrayed as Black. In a later section, we'll revisit the concept of the Earth mother as a Black woman.

ADAM, THE ORIGINAL MAN

In the Hebrew Bible, Adam's name can be traced back to root words that suggest "earth." The word *'adamah* can denote a red or reddish-brown clay that was common in the area, suggesting that the Biblical Adam was understood to be a "hued man." In the Qur'an, however, (15: 26-28), Adam is made from "black mud," suggesting that early Muslims accepted that the original man was a Black man.

In either case, Adam is described as one who inherits the "breath" or spirit of the Hebrew God, or who succeeds the Islamic God as his vicegerent. Both traditions suggest that the original man carries some degree of God in his incarnation.

WHAT IS RUAKH?

Did you know that the words "breath" and "spirit" are closely connected? This is why words you'll find words like "respiration" (meaning breathing) having the same root word as "spirit" and "inspiration." This goes back to the Bible, where God is said to have breathed his spirit into man. The word used is *ruakh*.

Ruakh, in Hebrew, means both "breath" and "spirit." Like the Egyptian concept of *ka* or the Chinese *chi*, *ruakh* refers to the divine energy incarnate in man (or perhaps *as* man). It attests to the direct connection between the mind who created the universe and man himself. In fact, while we're talking etymology, we should note that "man" means *mind*, another illustration of this dynamic.

We explore this concept in depth in *The Science of Self, Volume One*. We'll also revisit it in a future book, *The Hidden Tradition*.

THE GODS OF AFRICA

FROM THE AKAN TO THE ZULU

"The concept of a Black God is also found in all African religions." – Pan-African Journal, 1973

If we're going to talk about Black gods, it would be insane to ignore Africa. Yet in many books, even those focusing on Black history, indigenous African traditions are either ignored or glossed over to make room for everyone's favorite civilization: ancient Egypt.

In this section, we'll discuss many of the gods of ancient Egypt, exploring what they represent and how they came to be worshipped, but we'll also explore the rich traditions of Africa beyond Egypt.

THE GODS OF EGYPT

Godfrey Higgins once declared that all of the gods and goddesses of Greece were originally Black because they were derived from the divinities of Egypt, all of whom were as Black as the ancient Egyptians themselves.

According to Senegalese Egyptologist Cheikh Anta Diop, the Nile Valley's "good gods" were always depicted as Black, while the "bad gods" were portrayed with red skin or other coloring. While these gods could symbolize the forces of nature, Diop says they may have also been men who sprang from the Egyptian race itself and were deified as national heroes.

In this section, we'll look at some of the deities of the Nile Valley.

ATUM THE CREATOR

Let's begin with one of the gods who many ancient Egyptians regarded as the "first God." You may not have ever heard of him, but Atum is one of the most important and frequently mentioned gods in ancient Egyptian cosmology. In the Pyramid Texts, he is portrayed as both the Creator and father to the king, both roles of paramount importance. He was also considered the "father of the gods." Later, he was associated with the Sun.

But Atum wasn't worshipped by all Egyptians. As you may know, different parts of the Nile Valley had different traditions. The worship of Atum was primarily based out of the city of Heliopolis.

In the Heliopolitan creation myth, Atum was the first god, having created himself from the primordial waters of triple darkness (called *Nun*). He then spit out Shu (god of air) and Tefnut (goddess of moisture). When these two went out into the primordial waters, he sent his eye (later known as the "Eye of Ra") out after them. When they were found, he named Shu "life" and Tefnut "order" and entwined them together.

Shu and Tefnut gave birth to the earth (Geb) and the sky (Nut) who in turn gave birth to Osiris, Isis, Set, and all the other deities, each of whom – in this tradition – symbolized a law of physics or nature.* Through them, the universe came to be what it is today.

What's amazing about the Heliopolitan myth is how closely it corresponds with reality. That is, this symbolic language of myth and metaphor is shockingly close to what modern physicists have discovered about the actual formation of our universe.[91] We explore this process in depth in *The Science of Self, Volume One*. How did the ancient Egyptians know all this? What more did they know?

Atum, as the "transcendent" source of all existence, is rarely depicted in human form. He was usually depicted as a crown or as

---

* In other traditions, these deities were derived from the stories of founders, leaders, teachers, and other important personalities.

one of his many totem animals, most often of which was a black bull carrying the sun disk between his horns. When he is pictured in human form, however, Atum is a Black man wearing a headdress or crown like that of the Pharaohs. Some theologians suggest that the name of *Atum*, the "original man," was related to a later tradition, that of the Hebrew *Adam*.

THE SUN GOD RA

Atum was a solar deity, associated with the sun god Ra, in the form of a composite god known as Atum-Ra. Ra (also written as Re) was often considered to be the King of the Gods. The ancient Egyptians didn't actually

Ra

worship the sun, but they worshipped Ra, who they saw personified in the Sun. Sound confusing? I'll explain.

Ra was associated with creating the world and fathering humanity, and he once lived on Earth where he was the king of all – gods and men alike. But it was believed he had become an "old man," and humans began questioning his judgement. A tired and frustrated Ra then withdrew to the sky. He appointed other gods to maintain order on Earth, a responsibility that then passed to human successors – the Pharaohs, who were considered the "sons of Ra."

Ra is traditionally pictured as dark-skinned man wearing a falcon mask with a sun disk above it. In some areas, the worship of Ra was combined with Atum, where the god was known as Atum-Ra. In Thebes, he was associated with Amen as Amen-Ra.

AMEN, THE HIDDEN GOD

When people say "Amen" at the end of a prayer, they're actually showing respect to an Egyptian god. Amen was a "high god"

Amen

worshipped across Egypt, and his worship quickly spread into the Near East, where the Judaic traditions developed.

Amen was one of the eight gods created by Ra to govern the Earth in the beginning. According to Revelation 3:14, Amen is "the beginning of the creation of God." When Hebrew communities said Amen, they were invoking the unseen power of their God. In Egypt, Amen meant "The Hidden One."

Amen-Ra

At first, Amen may have been worshipped locally at Thebes, but after he was combined with Ra as Amen-Ra, he became the primary god of all Egypt. His worship soon spread far beyond the Nile Valley. He was even known by the Greeks, who called Zeus by the name Ammon. In various texts, Amen is often written Amon. But as Sir William Drummond wrote in 1825, "The difference between A man, Amen, and Amon is nothing. The Egyptians in ancient times probably, I may say certainly, often omitted vowels, like the Hebrews and Arabs."[92]

Amen is traditionally pictured as a bearded Black man, wearing a headdress topped by two tall plumes of feathers.

OSIRIS, LORD OF THE PERFECT BLACK

For beginners, Osiris (whose names is better translated as Ausar), one of the chief deities of the Egyptian pantheon, was called "Lord of the Perfect Black." As I explain in *When the World was Black,* Ausar was based on a real leader:

As the Egyptians consolidated, the extent of their empire gradually expanded to cover larger stretches of the north. This is reflected in their myths, which recall a migration coming from the south. In fact, according to Cheikh Anta Diop, not only was Ausar (Osiris) once a real historical personality, he is the one credited with leading the ancestors of the Egyptians out of Nubia. Diop, a reputable historian, anthropologist, and physicist, even declared that Ausar's actual head was preserved in a canopic jar discovered at Abydos![93]

In other words, Ausar was based primarily on an actual human figure. Others, like Atum, Ra, and Amen, were based on the "transcendent" consciousness that fashioned the universe. Ausar was also connected to natural principles (like fertility and agriculture), but his myth might have been based directly on an actual Black man who led the ancestors of the Egyptians into Egypt, where they quickly developed a strong agricultural tradition.

If Atum, Ra, and Amen, were also based on historical people, these people must have lived long before the time of Ausar. If that's the case, we won't find traces of these individuals in the Nile Valley. We'll have to look at the indigenous "inner" African communities where the Egyptians came from.

Osiris

FROM INNER AFRICA, NOT ASIA

Why do Egyptologists attempt to trace everything in the Nile Valley back to the Near East?

Simple. Because, the ancient Near East is not seen as an indigenous Black area (even though it was). The goal is to associate the Near East with people who look Caucasian, and to make ancient Egypt out to be the work of white people. They'd rather promote these civilizations as the work of ancient aliens over admitting that it was an indigenous African development.

Some scholars have even said that the gods of Egypt were derived from those of the Near East and Europe, rather than the other way around. Fortunately, scholars like Ivan Van Sertima and Cheikh Anta Diop have worked tirelessly to refute these claims. Recently, linguist and historian Christopher Ehret has written:

It is doubtful whether Osiris can be regarded as equal to Tammuz or Adonis, or whether Hathor is related to the "Great Mother." There are closer relations with northeast African religions. The numerous animal cults (especially bovine cults and panther gods) and details of ritual dresses (animal tails, masks, grass aprons, etc) **probably are of African origin**.

The kinship in particular shows some African elements, such as the king as the head ritualist (i.e., medicine man), the limitations and renewal of the reign (jubilees, regicide), and the position of the king's mother (a matriarchal element).[94]

Ehret says some of these traditions can be traced back to Ethiopians south of Egypt, and others to "Prenilotic tribes" like Shilluk. In other words, the Black gods and goddesses of ancient Egypt were derived from indigenous Black men and women in Africa.

THOTH, THE GOD OF WISDOM

Thoth was the Egyptian god of wisdom and learning. His name is better translated as Djehuti. The Greeks called him Hermes and the Romans knew him as Mercury, the messenger of the Gods. Later, the European students of Hermetic philosophy came to know him as *Hermes Trismegistus*, or "Hermes, three times great."

In our modern edition of *The Kybalion*, I write:

The Egyptians credited Djehuti as the inventor of language and the author of all works of science, theology, philosophy, and esoteric knowledge. When the Greeks adopted his worship they identified him, as Hermes, as the inventor of astronomy, astrology, medicine, botany, theology, government, geometry, reading, writing, and public speaking. Hermes had not only created the numbers and the alphabet, the Greeks believed, but had given them their secret meanings.

As Muslims had identified Hermes with Idris, the Greeks said Hermes had taught Pythagoras, one of their first scientists (who had indeed studied in Egypt) everything he knew. They claimed he was the true author of every work of every branch of knowledge, human and divine. Much of this can be traced back to Greek perceptions of Egyptian cosmology.

Djehuti played many vital and prominent roles in Egyptian mythology, and was thus associated with a variety of symbols and principles. The ancient Egyptians regarded him as self-begotten and self-made. He is credited with making the calculations for the establishment of the heavens, the Earth, and everything in the visible Universe. Without his words, the Egyptians believed, the gods would not exist. In the underworld, he was A'an, the god of equilibrium. His feminine counterpart, Ma'at, was the force which maintained balance and order. With Ma'at, Djehuti maintained the Universe, on both the moral (human) and cosmological scales.[95]

On the cover of our edition of *The Kybalion*, we feature a painted relief of Djehuti, where he is shown next to Pharoah Seti I. Although the god is wearing his traditional ibis mask, his skin is clearly dark brown, matching the complexion of the African pharaoh, Seti I. The ancient Egyptians understood Djehuti as a Black god, as they did all of their other deities.

PTAH, THE MASTER BUILDER

Robert Halliburton says "the oldest type of the divinity in Egypt was that of Ptah, the Creator," and that he was identified by the Greeks with Hephaistos, "the Architect of the Universe." Ptah was not worshipped across all of Egypt, but his cult was centered in the city of Memphis. According to the Memphite Theology, Ptah was the Creator:

Bes

> Thus it is said of Ptah: 'He who made all and created the gods.' And he is Ta-tenen, who gave birth to the gods, and from whom every thing came forth, foods, provisions, divine offerings, all good things. Thus it is recognized and understood that he is the mightiest of the gods. Thus Ptah was satisfied after he had made all things and all divine words.[96]

Ptah, as a Creator, was the patron god of craftsmen, associated with stone-working. He was depicted as a bearded Black man standing upright, but wrapped up like a mummy, with his hands free only to hold a scepter representing life, power, and stability.

BES, PATRON GOD OF CHILDBIRTH

In *Ancient Egypt: The Light of the World*, acclaimed British historian Gerald Massey discusses the god Bes, who is worshipped as a protector of households, and in particular, of mothers and children (and childbirth). He was said to be jolly, fond of music, humor, and dancing. Gerald Massey describes him as a "negroid Pygmy."

Bes was a lot like the "lucky gods" that are found in homes across Japan and China, as Massey explains:

> He had no temples and no priesthood other than his oracle, but statues or depictions of the god was found in most homes throughout the land of Egypt. Although not originally one of the more famous of the gods, Bes came to be loved by the people of Egypt. It was the dwarf god-demon Bes that they came to call on for protection in their daily lives.[97]

As BBC journalist Alaistar Sooke explains, Bes was "tremendously popular in ancient Egypt." He was worshipped by the common people, who associated him "with many of the good things in life: sex, drinking, music, and merriment."

PROVIDING PROTECTION FOR PROSTITUTES?

Knowing this might help you understand the following. We've all heard that the world's oldest profession is prostitution.

Massey continues:

> As another form of protection, an image of the dwarf god was tattooed on some women – different depictions of women, such as girls swimming, female dancers, acrobats and musicians, show them with Bes painted on their skin. The women with the image of Bes tattooed on her upper thigh around the pubic area might be sacred 'prostitutes', the tattoo being used to ward off venereal disease. This was probably because of his association with music and entertainment, as well as being a protector of women and children. It could have also been a tattoo relating to sexuality or fertility.

The Bes Tattoo

Before you think too negatively about prostitutes with Bes tatted on their thighs, keep in mind that many ancient gods were like the "patron saints" of the sex trade. Even Jesus kept the company of one or two. Whatever you make of all this, Massey doesn't skip a beat and jumps right into Bes' African origins:

> He was not a god of Egyptian origin. Bes was described as 'Coming from the Divine Land' and 'Lord of Punt' (perhaps an area in present day Somalia – see Hatshepsut's Expedition to Punt). He was thus linked to the goddess Hathor who was known as the 'Lady of Punt' and also a goddess of music… He comes capering into Egypt along with the Great Mother, Apt, from Puanta in the far-off south.[98]

This could explain why Bes is often depicted as a pygmy, or a member of the DBP (Diminutive Black People). Massey adds that "pygmies" were held in high regard throughout the Nile Valley:

> In Egypt, there are examples of dwarfs living in Egypt – from Seneb, who was rich enough to afford a tomb where he is shown with his normal sized wife and child, to personal attendants in the royal family, to entertainers and jesters. Other examples of dwarfs were a predynastic drawing of the "Dwarf Zer" from Abtu (Abydos) and a 5th Dynasty statuette of Khnumhotep from Saqqara. It seems that dwarfs were accepted members of Egyptian society, and they possibly had an important part in the Egyptian religion, being linked with Bes.

These people were found far beyond northeast Africa. In 1900, a study cites the Lama of Tibet having attendants who "are black with curly negroid hair, and some are dwarfs."[99] DBP people were high regarded throughout Africa, Asia, Europe, and North America.

Pygmy Gods?

Professor Sayce, commenting on Herodotus's third *Book of History*, says that Ptah was also represented as a dwarf. Gerald Massey connects Bes and Ptah as "pygmy" gods:

> In reality, Bes-Horus is the earliest form of the Pygmy Ptah. In both the dwarf is the type of man in his most primitive shape. The seven powers that co-operate with Ptah are also represented as seven Pygmies. Thus the anthropomorphic type comes into view as a Pygmy!

Massey is saying that Ptah and Bes represent the world's first people, who are also the world's first gods:

> The one sole race that can be traced among the aborigines all over the earth, above ground or below, is the dark race of a dwarf negrito type, and the only one possible motherland on earth for these preliminary people is Africa. No other country possesses the necessary background as a basis for the human beginnings. And so closely were the facts of nature observed and registered by the Egyptians that the earliest divine men in their mythology are portrayed as Pygmies...
>
> In this way the Egyptian wisdom registers the fact that the Pygmy was the earliest human figure known, and that this was brought into Egypt from the forests of Inner Africa and the record made in the mythology. In this mode of registering the natural fact the Egyptians trace their descent from the folk who were the first in human form – that is, from the Pygmies.[100]

Bes Becomes the Devil

Bes's origins may have been in Nubia or deeper within the African continent, but his worship quickly spread far beyond African shores. Alaister Sooke continues:

> By the end of the second millennium BC, Bes had proliferated across the Mediterranean world. Even local, non-Egyptian craftsmen produced objects decorated with his image. Early in the first millennium, the Phoenicians became big fans of Bes, as the Romans would too. Bes occasionally appears dressed as a Roman legionnaire. His rampant popularity even survived the advent of Christianity.

What happened next is telling. Visually, Bes was an odd character. Unlike other Egyptian deities, he wasn't portrayed in a side profile. Rather, images of him featured him facing the viewer, looking as if he was part pygmy, part lion, and yet all African. It was said that he could make babies laugh by making funny faces.

This "funny face," however, along with his impish gait, small stature, and an occasional lion's tail, were not well-received in the Christian world where he eventually arrived. The African god's features soon became the prototype for what many Christians now believe the devil looks like.

It began with the Greeks. "We know that little amulets of Bes were exported all over the eastern Mediterranean," says Anja Ulbrich, a curator at the Ashmolean Museum in Oxford. "So people definitely knew the image of Bes, and it may have influenced depictions of Greek demons and satyrs." These images were, in turn, absorbed by the Christian church. "The Christian faith had to compete with a lot of well-loved religions and cults," Ulbrich explains. "So it demonised them."

Sooke concludes his article on Bes as a forebear of the Christian devil with the following:

> To the ancient Egyptians, Bes was a friendly, protective god. Yet the Christians cast him as alien and disturbing in order to demonstrate the triumph of the new faith over older customs. So next time you find yourself considering an artistic representation of the Devil – such as Giotto's bearded, pot-bellied monster munching on sinners

in the Arena Chapel in Padua – spare a thought for his art-historical forefather, Bes. If nothing else, Bes teaches us that appearances can be deceptive.[101]

For more on how Blacks became devils, see the section on Sri Lanka, the section on Ahura Mazda, and the section on Job and his adversaries.

KING ZOSER WAS GODBODY

In ancient Egypt, most kings (known as Pharaohs) were venerated as living gods. This tradition appears to be as old as the Egyptian royalty itself, suggesting that great men and women were always considered divine. This didn't mean that every common person in the Nile Valley was considered a god, however. Instead, this

King Zoser

knowledge was a privilege afforded almost exclusively to the royalty and those who ascended to the priesthood via ancient Egypt's "mystery schools."

In other words, one had to be initiated to be recognized as a god or goddess. It simply wasn't something that the farmer in district 87 just chose to do for themselves. Of course, the ancient Egyptians weren't the only ones to make this knowledge exclusive. As you'll learn in the follow-up to this book, *theosis* was historically not for everyone, but for the elite.

It's not until 1960s Harlem, when the founder of the Five Percenters began teaching Black men that they were all God (with no sort of "rank" or hierarchy) that we find a truly socialist system for this knowledge being shared publicly. By the 80s, you could find brothers on street corners everywhere, coming up with creative ways to express the fact that they were God in the flesh. One of those terms, "godbody," quickly became popularized by Hip Hop.

What's this got to do with Egypt? I'll explain. Over 5,000 years ago, a king named Narmer founded the ancient Egypt dynasties by uniting upper and lower Egypt under one empire. After Narmer (who is always portrayed with strong African features), we don't know much about the kings of Egypt until the reign of Zoser (sometimes written Djoser) in the 3rd dynasty (c. 2687 BC).

By this time, many of the technological accomplishments of the civilization were already in place. But Zoser is worthy of note because he is associated with a major marvel in Egyptian history. He's the one who commissioned high priest Imhotep to engineer the construction of the step pyramid at Sakkara, widely recognized as **the world's first large-scale, cut-stone construction**. There were structures that resembled pyramids before this, but nothing close to this scale.

In any statue you'll find of Pharaoh Zoser, his features are undeniably African. Zoser was most definitely a Black man. What's worth noting is that this brother was called *Netjerikhet* by his contemporaries. *Netjerikhet* literally translates as "godbody," predating the Five Percenters' use of the term by 3500 years.

THE GODS OF THE MASAI

The Masai are an indigenous people of East Africa. There, they have a strong reputation as formidable warriors, with men who chase lions (rather than the other way around!) *single-handedly* as a rite of passage into adulthood. Until the British wiped out their military with infectious diseases, the Masai were beating them senseless.

They have a rich and ancient cultural tradition, developed over thousands of years of settlement in East Africa, long before foreigners came.

A NATURAL CULTURE

In *The Last of the Masai*, Sidney Hinde writes:

> Though the Masai cannot lay claim to any definite form of religion, they possess a more marked ethical instinct than is usually associated with primitive peoples. This is instanced both in their laws and in the sense of justice common to the race…Masai belief postulates annihilation after death, and unless a man has children to continue his name he is completely forgotten.[102]

Hinde's perspective is Eurocentric, but he admits that the Masai are no "savages." And the religion of the Masai isn't so much of a "religion" as it is an ethical culture with shared traditions, stemming back thousands of years. Their understanding of whether a man lives after he physically dies is also an interesting precursor to the culture of the Five Percenters, who have traditionally shared the same view.

The Masai aren't strict materialists, however. That is, they recognize that there is more to life than meets the eye, and that there is something almost incomprehensible beneath the surface of what we perceive as reality. Hinde continues:

> Ngai ("the Unknown") embodies their apprehension of power beyond human faculties of coping with. Thunderstorms, rains, the telegraph, a railway-engine, are all referred to as Ngai; and the word represents the incomprehensible, of which they are vaguely conscious.[103]

Thus, *Ngai* is much like the divine energy we talk about elsewhere in the book as *ruakh*, *chi*, and *ka*.* Ngai is inherent in life and nature, and incarnate in the Masai. The name Ngai. Engai means God.

ENGAI NAROK

Engai Narok is the Supreme God of the Masai. He is always described as a Black god. But he is not alone. Nor is he "unknown." Luke Plunkett writes:

> Another belief of the Masai is that there are two gods – a black one and a red one, the former being good and the latter malevolent. The spiritual function of the black god (Engai narok), who is kind and benevolent, is to send rain in order that the grass may grow to feed their flocks, while the red god (Engai nanyokye) endeavors to prevent the rain to kill them.[104]

Can you see the connections with the Egyptian mythology surrounding Ausar (or Osiris) and Set (or Seth)? These two are also black and red, with Ausar representing the life-giving Nile and its fertile black soil, and Set representing the encroaching desert sand to the west of the Nile.

But these personalities did not ONLY represent the duality of nature. They were also associated with groups of people. Set was associated with white people, known as the Temehu, who lived in the deserts and marshes west of the Nile. On the other hand, Ausar was considered an ancestor or former leader of the Black people of the Nile Valley.

Similarly, the blackness of Engai can be associated with dark rain clouds, but, as Sir Harry Hamilton Johnson proposed in 1904, there's

---

* These concepts are explored in depth in *The Hidden Tradition*, also from Supreme Design Publishing.

also a very human character to this Black god:

> The black god was very human in his attributes – and, in fact, was nothing but a glorified man, and the ancestor of the Masai. They generally imagine that the black god originally lived on the snowy summit of Mount Kenya, where the other gods, pitying his loneliness, sent him a small boy as a companion. When the boy grew up, he and the black god took to themselves wives from amongst the surrounding Negro races, and so procreated the first Masai men. Afterwards, the grey and the red gods became angry at the increase of people on the earth, and punished the world with a terrible drought and scorching heat. The child-companion of the black god, who had grown up into a man and was already the father of several Masai children, started off for the sky to remonstrate with the deities. A few days afterwards he returned, bringing copious rain with him, and remained henceforth on earth till his own death at a ripe age.[105]

In other words, Engai was thought to have once been a flesh-and-blood Black man, not solely a principle of nature.

NAITERU-KOP

The Masai recognized other Black gods as well:

> Besides the black and red gods, the Masai hold in veneration a certain quasi-divine personage named Naiteru-kop. He is apparently a kind of deified man and is supposed to dwell amidst the snow on Mount Kilimanjaro. His power is by no means as great as Engai, and although regarded as their Adam, he is not the creator, but merely the arranger of the present order of things in the world.
>
> Naiteru-kop is said to have obtained by some means a child, whom he called Le-eyo. This child when he grew up to be a man had two sons, the younger of which became the founder of the Masai tribe, whilst the elder, having lost his birthright—like the eldest son of Isaac—became the ancestor of the other inferior tribes. It was, they say, through an act of disobedience on the part of Le-eyo that death first entered into the world.[106]

Could *Naiteru* derive from the Egyptian *neteru* (or "gods")? It's possible. Either way, the similarities to the ancient Egyptian cosmology are many.

CHANGING TRADITIONS

However, since these traditions were recorded over 100 years ago, much has changed. As early as 1915, it was clear that much of the Masai's cosmology was being lost. Plunkett's summary is especially revealing:

Moreover, those parts of the continent that have come under European sway may be said to be, at the present time, in a state of transition. Already there are signs **that the younger generation of the tribes** in Equatorial Africa that have been brought in contact with outsiders, whether Europeans or Asiatics, **are losing interest in the old order of things.**

Many, fortunately, are embracing Christianity; others, not a few, are being seduced into the creed of Islamism. At any rate, **old manners and customs are dying out, ancient observances are being forgotten by the grim utilitarianism of modern times and by pressure from the white man.** Hut taxes and poll taxes have to be paid, public roads and bridges have to be constructed – and the white man insists on fairly honest service being given before he pays wages – leaving in consequence little time, for example, for the mourning period of from 3 to 6 months spent in lamentation for a deceased chief, as was the custom in bygone days.[107]

Who will preserve these oral traditions? Who will tell these stories? Who will keep the knowledge of our ancestors alive? Who, if not us?

GOD AS MAN ACROSS AFRICA

John Mbiti, in his *Concepts of God in Africa,* makes the gross generalization that "African peoples do not consider God to be a man,"[108] and promotes a scholastic trend we also encounter among the early interpreters of Native American mythology and religion, that is, accepting that these peoples view God as a "Great Spirit" only, and not a corporeal [physical] deity.

This idea was most likely introduced to both populations by Christian missionaries who doubled as early anthropologists, both describing native beliefs while simultaneously supplanting them with their own. As a result, we – in reading the works that have followed – tend to see indigenous thought through white eyes. Even isolated indigenous societies themselves – after centuries of missionary influence – have substantially different conceptions of the divine than they did before European contact.

Yet this is certainly not true of all African populations. Many are very clear about their long-standing God-concepts, which are not at all immaterial, invisible, and indescribable. Instead, many of the supreme gods, or "high gods" as some anthropologists label them, are depicted as Black men who, though they are often human in appearance, display both transcendent and human qualities.

THE GOD WHO IS FAR

The God who created the heavens and earth is not always described abstractly. "Transcendence" is ascribed to God in terms of him transcending time, space, knowledge, and ability, all measures in which this God has no limits.

But such accounts, where the God of all is infinite, supreme, and all-knowing, do not suggest to African people that this God cannot also exist as a physical being, recognized in very human terms. After all, a God with no limitations would not be limited from appearing to humans as a fellow human. This is where we find that God can be both "far" and "near."

In *Concepts of God in Africa*, John Mbiti writes:

> The transcendence of God is a difficult attribute to grasp, and one which must be balanced with God's immanence [nearness to men]...Many foreign writers constantly harp on the note that for African peoples God is "too remote" and virtually excluded from human affairs. This assertion is false, and the many facts contained in this book show clearly that people consider God to be both "far" and "near." [109]

Throughout Africa, as in many other parts of the world, the Creator may be "removed" from mortal affairs, but he is also known to inhabit the Earth, living among men. This is where find the "immanent" (or near) aspect of the "anthropomorphic" God.

WHAT IS ANTHROPOMORPHISM?

In terms of religion, "anthropomorphic" simply means that God is described having human qualities. Of course, to simply say that God speaks, moves, or displays emotion is contrary to the idea of an immaterial, nonhuman "Great Spirit" and instead suggests a more human deity. But the most anthropomorphic traditions go much further, describing God as a living, breathing, walking Black man.

THE GOD WHO IS NEAR

The Adinkra Gye Nyame

"Our God is black
Black of eternal blackness
With large voluptuous lips
Matted hair and brown liquid eyes...
For in his image we are made.
Our God is black."
— Togolese writer R.A. Armattoe[110]

What is God like in his immanent

aspect? That is, how have African people described God as one who was flesh and blood, like them?

WHAT DOES GOD LOOK LIKE?

The Lugbara hold God to be primarily invisible, though he may become visible to a person near death. In his visible form, Mbiti remarks that "people think of him anthropomorphically, believing that as Adro [his immanent aspect] he comes into direct contact with his creatures on earth...and is then said to have a human body which is split in the middle and 'very terrible to see.'"[111]

As stated before, the somewhat commonly accepted idea of the invisibility of God does not mean that he is impossible to see, but rather that few, or none, have seen him and lived. This view is held among the Bambuti, Lugbara, Vugusu, and others.

The Suk are more explicit in saying that "long, long ago, old men who now are dead, saw God in form of a man with huge wings whose flapping causes thunder and lightning."[112]

The Meru address him in prayer as "One Body and Possessor of strength."[113]

Among the Shilluk, one report says God "is from one side spirit, and from the other side spirit, but from front and back he is body."

The Aushi imagine him as a person, "to be small – about two feet in height – black and hard like stone."[114]

GOD IS A TRAVELING MAN

African gods are described sleeping, sitting, eating, drinking, breathing, walking the earth, and engaged in many other human activities. Robert P. Scharlemann describes the Yoruba as "very anthropomorphic about their concept of God,"[115] adding that, while he is transcends mortality, he "can be invoked to act like human beings."

The Yoruba supreme god, addressed primarily as Olorun, was once challenged by the sea god Olokun to a contest where "[t]he winner would be the god with the finest clothes."[116] Finally, while Olorun is the common name for God among the Yoruba, it is often used interchangeably with another of his names, Oluwa. Scharlemann comments, "The name Oluwa also appears to show the Deity as a person. He has life, consciousness, and knowledge. He is always active and acting in the world."[117]

God is believed, in many cases to be quite remote, though he visits the Earth on occasion, at which time he uses a very human form. The Jumjum think that God "sits on a horse" when he travels, while the Gad call God by the name Dzemawon "because he walks around the world and the towns."

The Lango believe that there are certain paths where God always walks, and people avoid building their homes nearby.

According to the Luvedu, when God created man, he left his footprints on rocks that were still soft, where they remain today.[118]

When there is an earthquake, the Bambuti say, "The Lord is taking a walk." The same belief is held by the Shone who think that God walks in earthquakes.

THE HOME OF GOD

As a rule, the great majority of traditional African religions portray God as having initially cohabited the earth with man until one day removing himself to some remote abode, be it the heavens above or the elevated, or simply isolated, regions of the Earth.

The Gikuyu have five sacred mountains that they consider the resting places of God when he visits the earth. This "mountain abode" is a popular belief across Africa, which may have something to do with the belief in his "remoteness."

The Bavenda claim God "manifests himself" in the Matoba hills, while the Jumjum claim it is Jebel Tunya where God resides (and so no one goes there), and the Meru claim that Mount Kenya is the "earthly abode of God."[119]

Among the Bambuti, God is said to have, at first, actually lived with the first people (two sons and a daughter), though he would never show himself. He "lived in a big house" and supplied man with all that he needed, warning, however, that man should never seek him out. The story continues thus:

> The daughter's duty was to draw water and fetch firewood for him, placing them at the door of his house, from where God took them in without being seen by the children. This happy and close relationship ended one day when the daughter was overcome by curiosity and tried to watch God as he took in the pot of water. She hid herself nearby and saw him "stretch forth his arm, which was well covered with brass rings, outside his abode, to take in the pot. She had seen it – the richly adorned arm of God. How her heart rejoiced! But alas! Her sin was immediately followed by punishment."[120]

As follows, things would not be the same once God had been seen. However, in this case, the result was not death, but God's withdrawal from man. Mbiti adds, "Since then no one has seen him."[121]

GOD THE FATHER, EARTH THE MOTHER

This God is often regarded as a father figure, being addressed specifically as "Father" or "Grandfather" (the tribe calling on him usually being his children or grandchildren). This "old man" as numerous peoples view him, is in many cases a "Great Ancestor" to the people who acknowledge him.

It should be said that African cultures are typically not as patriarchal as Western culture. That is, things are more balanced between men and women. In many cases, family trees are matrilineal, meaning they are based on your mother, not your father.

In traditional African society, women also have a much higher social standing than in many Western cultures. With that said, the Creator God is typically not describes as feminine, but masculine. This isn't meant to denigrate women, but it most likely stems from the understanding gender roles in procreation. Female deities are described as the Earth, the Moon, the fertile soil, or a maternal figure who bears, nourishes and sustains life.

There is, of course, no life without her. But, in most African traditions, the Earth is the mother, and God is the father.

Thus God is often referred to as "Father." Communities such as the Nuer who call God "Our Father" and regard him as a "a living person" hold this view, as do the Lunda, Bemba, Suk, Ganda, Banyoro, Chawai, Urhobo, Nuba, Sonjo, Bambuti, Azande, Teso, and countless others.[122]

The majority of these people regard themselves as the children of God, and God, in turn, is often seen literally as being the Father of mankind, sometimes as a direct parent of the original man. According to Mbiti:

> God and the original man were in a very close relationship. Some peoples picture God as living among men or visiting them from time to time. It was a family relationship in which God was the parent and the men were the children.[123]

This Father god is very human among a large number of peoples. Some of the communities who regard God as having (or having had) a wife (or wives), and children, include the Bushmen, Lozi, Ila, Madi, Zulu, and Edo peoples. Mbiti adds, "in the Herero double name for God, *Ndjambi Karunga*, the latter is the earthly aspect of God and in this he is married to one wife, with two or three children." The immanent Lugbara God is said to have "wives and many children."[124]

GOD AS AN OLD MAN

God in is described as elderly, old, or ancient, and the titles "elder," "grandfather," and "old man" are used in the same context as "Father" when referring to the Deity. Among the Temne, God is known as *Kurumusaba*, which means "old" or "ancient."[125]

The name of the Zulu God, *Unkulunkulu* means "Old, Old, One."[126] This God was said to be "both the first man and the creator. A god of the earth who…showed men how to live together and gave them knowledge of the world in which they lived."[127] You can look back to the section on the "Old Man" of Native American cosmologies to see the similarities between their accounts.

GOD AS AN ANCESTOR

J.B. Danquah, in his *Akan Doctrine of God,* says that the "doctrine" of God in Africa can be summed up as "the cult of God as the Great Ancestor, with all other Ancestors in between as Mediators."[128] It was Herbert Spencer who proposed that ancestor-worship was the root-form of all Gods, and Danquah's statement lends support to this perspective.

The Yoruba are said to have "sprung from Lamurudu, one of the kings of Mecca whose offsprings were: Oduduwa, the ancestor of the Yorubas, the kings of Gogobiril and of the Kukawa, two communities in the Hausa country."[129]

In other words, Lamurudu came from the east. At this time, "Mecca" could have referred to a city in Arabia or another nearby civilization, ancient Egypt. As we noted in *When the World was Black*, there's genetic, cultural, and linguistic evidence to suggest that some of the people of West African could have come from the east.

Ethnographer Samuel Johnson says Oduduwa was considered by the Ife to be the son of Oludumare (another name for the supreme god Olorun), and that they worship him to this day.[130] Were Oludumare (the supreme God) and Lamurudu (a human king and ancestor) one and the same? We can't be sure, but this account certainly asserts that the divinity of the Deity continues down a bloodline.

The Akan call their God "the Grand Ancestor" as well as "Grandfather 'Nyame' who alone is the Great one." It should be noted that Nyame translates best as "energy" (like Chi, Ruakh, Ka, etc.), suggesting that this divine energy transferred from the ultimate ancestor down to all of his descendants. The Gye Nyame symbol used by the Akan people represents God's presence in the world, signifying that God was here in the beginning, is active here now, and will be here when it is all over, knowing everything the entire time.

Nyankopon, another Akan name for God, is derived from the word Nyame. Nyankopon is also called Nana, which means "root, begetter or seed."[131] Again, the Akan are reminded of the energy that is in them, and where it ultimately comes from.

This is Harry Sawyerr's central argument in *God: Ancestor or Creator?* That is, the gods of Africa were (or are) persons deified. For example, "Among the Nyakyusa, the word for God, Kyala, derives from one of the hero-founders of the tribe."[132] Sawyerr produces a wealth of examples, documenting this tradition across Africa.

THE DEIFICATION OF LEADERS

Of course, not all gods were the "Supreme God." Some of these "lesser" gods were not based on the "ultimate ancestor," but on another important historical figure who became deified after death. According to one Yoruba myth:

Shango was the fourth king of the Yoruba people. He was such a tyrant, that two of his ministers challenged him for the throne. Shango had to flee into the forest where he wandered for a long time and, finally, hanged himself from a tree. After his death, his enemies' houses were set on fire, probably by Shango's friends. But some people believed Shango had gone up into the heavens and was sending fire down to Earth. Since then, Shango has been regarded as a storm-god, whose weapon was the ax, which represented the thunderbolt.[133]

Many former kings and leaders were made into gods, and some became revered as gods while they lived. The Yoruba give their king the title *Alaiye 'luwa*, which means the Chief, the man of ideal character and conduct who owns the world."[134]

Shango, Yoruba God and Orisha

The kings of the Zimba, Mbun, Lunda, Nyoro, Monomotapa, Nandi, Loango (where he was called *Sambee* and *Pango*, which mean God), Ganda (where a king once had the title *Llare*, which means "the Almighty One"), and many other African communities, were held to be gods, having control over the forces of nature and almost always having the power to make it rain upon command.[135] In some cases, the king was also allocated the power over life and death, as was the case with the king of Ruanda.

The king of Jukun was regarded as God incarnate. It was said he had power over nature, did not need to eat or sleep, and could not die. Of course, this is entirely reminiscent of the transcendent aspect of God. Called Aku, he had greater power over people than the sky-god Chido, "as a man could incur the wrath of Chido and live but who incurs the wrath of the Aku dies that very day."[136]

Further, both the king of Dahomej and Kaffitsho were regarded as living embodiments of the Deity. In Kaffitsho, the king was addressed by the title of the God *Heql*, a title also found in Ganda and Loango.[137]

As Julian Baldick explains in *Black God: The Afroasiatic Roots of the Jewish, Christian and Muslim Religions*:

> According to Onneken the Kafa king was indeed invisible to everyone except his closest entourage, and would receive visitors from behind a curtain. He would speak quietly, so that only his most trusted servants could hear him. The king was not allowed to apply his hands to any activity other than wielding arms. He always had to wear a gold bracelet on his right arm, a gold ring on one of his fingers, gold earrings and green clothing.

Mohammed Hassen, in his history of the Oromo, gives us more information about Kafa kings: they were not allowed to walk on the ground, and so cotton cloth had to be spread in front of them, and they could not touch their food, so that other people had to feed them.[138]

Back to that Invisible God

Did you make any connections above? Consider the transcendent aspect of God, where it is believed he does not sleep, eat or drink and therefore must have no need for such things. Consider this, however. If you take someone like a king, and you keep him unseen while spreading great stories about his power, what would happen?

The masses that have never seen him,

Mask of Alouroua, the "shy" or hidden Creator of the Baule people

but who have witnessed the effects of his rule (the construction of new roads, people receiving justice, etc.) could easily come to believe that this "god" was truly invisible and immortal. This is actually what has happened in recorded history.

In the case of the king of Jukun, for example, it was believed that he did not need to eat. Yet the reality was that when he did have a meal, it was simply said that he was "withdrawn."[139]

Imagine how much mystery could have surrounded our leaders and shamans over a thousand years ago. It's not hard to imagine powerful men and women being celebrated as immortals and unseen forces. What about the ancestors and hero-founders who were celebrated after death, and therefore referred to as having transcended to a higher place or "withdrawn" to somewhere remote and inaccessible (such as a mountain or the heavens above)?

MAN AS GOD IN AFRICA *

We've said quite a lot about God as Man, but what about the idea of Man as God? When we consider the Igbo concept of *chi*, the Zulu concept of *uqobo*, the Shona *mweyi*, the Bantu *muntu*, the Yoruba *ori*, and the Akan *okra* or *nyame*…we are looking at concepts of divine energy, where the Divine, the Creator, is incarnate in man himself. Or rather *as* man himself.†

This, however, wasn't the sort of idea that everyone talked about publicly. It wasn't necessarily even understood by everyone who participated in these traditions. In many cases, this knowledge only came to be fully understood through specialized education and training.

"Of a respected knower or a man who is master of himself people will say: "He's a Maa!": that is, a complete man." – Amadou Hampâté Bâ, African historian

In an important essay on the guardians of Africa's oral traditions, Amadou Hampâté Bâ writes:

> In Bambara, they are called domas or somas, the "knowers," or donikebas, "makers of knowledge." In Fulani, they are called, according to region, silatiquls, gandos, or tchioriknes, words which have this same sense of "knower".
>
> They may be Master Initiates (and Masters of Initiates) in one

---

* An excerpt from *The Hidden Tradition*, also from Supreme Design Publishing.

† For more on this, see "Conceptions of Self Across Cultures" in *The Science of Self, Volume One*.

particular traditional branch (initiations of the smith, the weaver, the hunter, the fisherman, etc.) or may possess complete knowledge of the tradition in all its aspects. Thus there are domas who know the blacksmith's science, the shepherd's, the weaver's, and there are also great initiation schools in the savannah in Mali, for instance, the Komo, the Kore, the Nama, the Do, the Diarra Wara, the Nya, the Nyawarole, and so on.

But let us make no mistake. African tradition does not cut life into slices and the knower is rarely a specialist. As a rule he is a generalist. For example, one and the same old man will be learned not only in plant science (the good or bad properties of every plant) but in earth sciences (the agricultural or medicinal properties of the different kinds of soil), and water sciences, astronomy, cosmogony, psychology, and so on. What is involved is a science of life in which knowledge can always be turned to practical use.

Keeper of the secrets of cosmic genesis and the sciences of life, the traditionalist, usually gifted with a prodigious memory, is often also the archivist of past events transmitted by tradition or of contemporary events.[140]

Until initiates received this kind of knowledge, all the gods and forces of nature were thought to be outside of self. After initiation, there was no self outside of God.

In *Africa and Africans*, Bohannan and Curtin write about what African initiation rituals truly represent:

Initiation is a ritual teaching to the novitiates that they embody, in themselves personally and in their relationships collectively, the moral force of society – they are themselves the gods...[141]

In other words, it wasn't just kings who became gods, because all power was not political. Often, priests, shamans, and others possessing advanced knowledge were given a "holy" or otherworldly status. For example, among the Moru people, members of the elite Bori clan were believed to contain God's spirit within them. The Moru said they possessed "special powers" and had access to "certain mystical forces."[142]

But initiation was a process, and all who succeeded were qualified to carry this title. They weren't yelling "I'm God" from their rooftops, yet those who understood knew what was what. For example, among the Bantu people, *Muntu* is the essence of man:

"Muntu" signifies then, vital force, endowed with intelligence and will. This interpretation gives a logical meaning to the statement which I one day received from a Bantu: "God is a great muntu." This meant "God is the great Person"; that is to say, *The* great, powerful and reasonable living force.[143]

In Mbiti's account of the Dogon, the explanation is more layered:

...the development of each person manifests ultimately the development of Nommo, "the appointed model of creation", "the symbol of the ordered word." The new-born baby is the head of Nommo; as herd-boy he is the chest of Nommo; at betrothal he is the feet of Nommo; at marriage he manifests the arms of Nommo; and when he is a full adult "he is the complete Nommo." Finally, as "an elder and still more as a supreme chief, he is both Nommo and the totality of the world and mankind." [144]

As you can see, deification was not an event, but a process. In this process, one did not become other than what he was. He simply became better acquainted with his true reality.

J.B. Danquah says Nana is "the pattern and paradigm – Mediator and Exemplar – of the Supreme Ideal."[145] Danquah begins his account of Akan cosmology by "presenting God as the sum-total of all human Nanas." By the end of his work, he leads us to the realization that Akan religion "in its highest expression is the worship of the race."[146] In other words, among the Akan and many other African traditions, the Black man is God. A very similar cosmology is found thousands of miles away, among the Five Percenters.

Take a break.
Put this book down for a minute.

Do NOT go back to reading this book until you do one (or more) of the following things:

- ☐ Call somebody who is going through some rough sh*t and make sure they are okay.
- ☐ Eat something that your body is telling you it needs, or drink some water.
- ☐ Wrestle, spar, or slapbox someone to make sure you "still got it."
- ☐ Take a walk through your neighborhood and see if somebody needs help with something.
- ☐ Clean up a part of your house, or organize some f*cked up part of your life.
- ☐ Tell somebody about this book and what you're learning. Invite them to come read it.
- ☐ Give this book away to somebody who needs it and get another copy for yourself.
- ☐ Cook something good, and make enough to share. Invite people.
- ☐ Check yourself out in the mirror and pick something to improve.
- ☐ Identify ten positive things about your life and stop forgetting them when you're stressed.
- ☐ Tell somebody you love them, cause it might be your last chance.

This has been a PSA from 360 and SDP.
Once you're done, carry on.

THE GODS OF EUROPE

FROM GREECE TO GREENLAND

"One would naturally suppose the color of a Deity would be the same as the complexion which belonged to the worshippers of it. Black Gods and Goddesses were met with among the Egyptians, Hindus, Greeks and Romans – yes, in Europe." – Abisha Hudson, 1889

Yes, in Europe. In fact, the people of Europe worshipped just as many Black gods as the rest of the world, until it seems that white Europeans changed their minds. There was certainly some white washing before then, but the spread of the Moorish occupation across Europe (711-1492 AD) led to a revival of sorts.

This period, where the ideas of European solidarity and white supremacy experienced a tremendous resurgence, is when we begin to see all of these Black gods and goddesses refashioned as white. This is, as we observed in our discussion of Jesus Christ, when Renaissance artists not only painted all of their Christian imagery in the palest of hues, but some also took great pains to repaint the darker images that existed already.

Abisha Hudson attests to the presence of these Black icons:

> There was a black Venus at Corinth. Osiris, Isis and her child Horus, were black. A black Virgin and black child are to be seen at St. Stephens, in Genoa; at St. Francisco, in Pisa; at St. Theodore, in Munich; and in other places.[147]

In some cases, these images were so highly revered that they could not be repainted without driving the local people into a panic. In *Anacalypsis,* Higgins remarked, "I once saw a man repainting a black God on a house-side in Italy." These images were holy enough to protect and preserve, and local Europeans took these commitments seriously.

As a result, these Black icons were not destroyed, but hidden away in vaults, catacombs, cathedral cellars, and – of course – within the Vatican's private collection, where many of them sit today.

THE GREEK GODS

You've already seen that Godfrey Higgins declared, almost 200 years ago, that the gods of Greece were most certainly derived from the Black gods of Egypt and Inner Africa. W.E.B. Du Bois echoed these sentiments, when he wrote that Egyptian civilization was African civilization "flourishing on the Nile but never separated from the great lakes of inner Africa."[148]

ISIS IN GREECE

In many cases, Greek historians acknowledge their immense cultural debt to the Egyptians and Ethiopians. In other cases, these transitions are recorded in myth. In the Greek myth of *The Golden Ass* (or *Metamorphosis*) by Apuleius, the author, as an initiate of the Isis cult, is told the following by Isis herself:

I am present; I who am Nature, the parent of things, queen of all the elements…the primitive Phrygians called me Pressimunitica, the mother or the gods; the native Athenians, Ceropian Minerva; the floating Cyprians, Paphian Venus…the inhabitants of Eleusis, the ancient goddess Ceres. Some again have invoked me as Juno, others as Bellona, others as Hecate, and others Rhamnusia; and those who are enlightened by the emerging rays of the rising sun, the Ethiopians, Ariians and Egyptians, powerful in ancient learning, who reverence by divinity with ceremonies perfectly proper, call me by my true appellation, Queen Isis.[149]

Hercules

HERCULES

You've heard of Hercules before. He was the legendary strong man who conquered everything in his path. He was considered semi-divine, having one parent who was a God and one who was a mortal. There are countless Greek myths attributed to Hercules and his exploits across Asia and Africa.

With that said, there's strong reason to think that Hercules was only later imagined to be a Greek, and that many of these tales were originally based on those of a Black man. Historian Josiah Priest has written:

> Respecting the Egyptians, Herodotus says, also, that Hercules was one of their gods, who was second only to Pan (the Creator) himself, in their estimation, and that from the Egyptians the Greeks

borrowed a knowledge of this god…

Herodotus was convinced that Hercules was truly a Tyrian, or a negro god, who was also the god of the Egyptians, the Ethiopians, and Lybians, as well as of ancient Babylon, of which empire Nimrod was the founder, although it passed into other hands in process of time…

Herodotus expressly says…that the Colchins and Egyptians, who were all one with the Tyrians, Zidonians, Ethiopians and Libyans, were black, and had short curling hair. **If such men were not negroes of the true stamp, we know not who are**…[150]

BLACK ATHENA

In more recent years, works like George G.M. James' *Stolen Legacy*, and Martin Bernal's *Black Athena*, have supported these arguments. In fact, the name of Bernal's book is based on fact the Greek goddess *Athena* is so closely connected to her Nile Valley roots that her name derives from that of her Egyptian prototype, the goddess *Neith*. Bernal's book has many strong points. But one of my favorite commentaries on this topic comes from a slightly older source.

FROM JUPITER TO JEHOVAH

In his 1939 work, *Ethiopia and the Origin of Civilization*, historian John G. Jackson says that the presence of Black gods throughout the world can suggest one of two things:

(1) the people there were once Black, or

(2) Blacks introduced this worship.

Jackson cites the Greek philosopher Xenophanes (572–480 B.C.) who said:

Neith

> Each man represents the gods as he himself is. The Ethiopian as black and flat-nosed the Thracian as red-haired and blue-eyed; and if horses and oxen could paint, they would no doubt depict the gods as horses and oxen.

Jackson adds:

> This being the case; when we find the great nations of the world, both past and present, worshipping black gods, then we logically conclude that these peoples are either members of the black race, or that they originally received their religion in total or in part from black people. The proofs are abundant. The ancient gods of India are shown with Ethiopian crowns on their heads.

According to the Old Testament, Moses first met Jehovah during his sojourn among the Midianites, who were an Ethiopian tribe. We learn from Hellenic tradition that Zeus, king of the Grecian gods, so cherished the friendship of the Ethiopians that he traveled to their country twice a year to attend banquets.

"All the gods and goddesses of Greece were black," asserts Sir Godfrey Higgins, "at least this was the case with Jupiter, Baccus, Hercules, Apollo, Ammon. The goddesses Benum, Isis, Hecate, Diana, Juno, Metis, Ceres, Cybele were black." Even the Romans, who received their religion mainly from the Greeks, admitted their debt to Egypt and Ethiopia.[151]

Let's recap. Jackson has just told us that the gods of India, Greece, and Rome, were derived from Blacks, and that even Jehovah himself must have originally been a Black god like the others. Rather than spend countless pages describing the massive Greek and Roman pantheons, I'll defer to the scholars who have shown that all of these deities were derived from the Egyptian and Ethiopian pantheons. The names and traits may have changed somewhat, but these gods and goddesses were originally Black.

THE DARK GODS OF EUROPE

As we explained in *When the World was Black*, the indigenous people of Europe were Black. In fact, National Geographic recently confirmed that Europe remained predominantly Black until about 6,000 years ago. Most of the original population were displaced, absorbed, or annihilated by the later arrivals who spoke Indo-European languages.

This is why Indo-European myths typically feature a "clash of the gods" where the primordial creations, described as dark dwarfs, giants, creatures, are demons (who represent the indigenous people), are conquered by "fair" gods and heroes. These people, of course, are meant to represent the whites who settled these areas, often by force, and later authored the myths that tell their stories.

By the time these myths become widespread, the Original people of the region were either gone, or had been pushed to the fringes of their old homeland. They survive mostly in myths, with a few genetic or linguistic survivals in the new population.

THE MAGICAL RACES

In *Fians, Fairies, and Picts*, David MacRitchie, a Scottish historian specializing in the myths and traditions of early Europe, explains how many of Europe's myths and legends of "magical races" developed:

> After a race has once disappeared from sight, the popular terms describing it must become more vague and confused with every century. Thus, in a certain traditional Scotch story there is mention of a number of "little black creatures with spades." The description is delightfully comprehensive. It would be quite applicable to a gang of Andaman coolies. On the other hand, if we exclude the "spades," it might be applied to any "little black creatures" – say a colony of tadpoles or of black-beetles. So that, when a poet or an artist gets hold of a tradition which has reached this stage of uncertainty, he may give the reins to his fancy, so long as he portrays some kind – any kind – of "little black creatures."[152]

In other words, it only takes a few generations for a story to go from an eyewitness account of history to a fanciful tale of magic and mystery. Here, we'll explore some of these stories and their origins.

BLACK GIANTS

Jack and the Beanstalk wasn't a true story, was it? Probably not. Early European myths of giants were based on men who were large and threatening, but not superhuman. The first men to be described as giants were Black men who came from overseas to rule.

In *Ancient and Modern Britons*, MacRitchie talks about these people and how they came to be described as giants:

> Such leaders, black of skin, savage in nature, and yet possessed of the evidences of a certain civilization (having jewels, gold ornaments, chessmen of gold, of ivory or of bone), are confusedly remembered in the popular traditions of Wales, of the Western Highlands, and probably of other portions of the United Kingdom.
>
> And these legendary tales, in many cases, reveal those savage chieftains as the kings, or reguli, or dukes of various neighbourhoods; in the centre of which is their stronghold. As, for example, the castle of the black "giant" Gwrnach, in the Welsh Mabinogion; or that of the Black Oppressor, or of the Black Knight of Lancashire; or, more historically, that of the Black Dubh-glass of Galloway – whose memory is still execrated in that territory.[153]

Elsewhere, MacRitchie notes an account of one Thorhall, who is said to be "a large man, and strong, black and like a giant, silent, and…a bad Christian," suggesting he was a "pagan."[154]

In another section, MacRitchie describes another giant myth and its likely origins:

> The tradition of Ettrick Forest bears, that the outlaw was a man of prodigious strength, possessing a batton or club, with which he laid

lee (i.e., waste) the country for many miles round." This account would give him a wilder aspect than that with which he is invested in the ballad, and suggests rather the characteristics of the "Black Murray" of Galloway, of the "big, black giant with a club," who figures in the popular tales of the Highlands and Wales, of the "Black Oppressor," whom Welsh Peredur slew, of the Black Knight of Lancashire, and of that particular Black Dubh-glass who is remembered, locally, as "one of the most horrible devils that ever appeared in Scotland" (being, perhaps, no other than the Black Morrow of the same neighbourhood, or of the same family). The club has always been a weapon of the "Moors" of Scotland – from the days of Severus down to our own; when "the bludgeon tribe" is used – in Galloway, at least – as a synonym for "the gypsies."[155]

Other stories of Black giants can be found in *African Presence in Early Europe*, edited by Ivan Van Sertima and Runoko Rashidi.

WHERE DO FAIRIES COME FROM?

When we think of fairies, we most likely think of Tinkerbell, the Tooth Fairy, and other childhood tales. The idea of "fairies" is commonly associated with the mythology of northern Europe, where you'll find beliefs involving sprites, pixies, gnomes, and all kinds of other tiny, magical beings. You may even be surprised to learn that many of the people living in the countries of northern Europe still believe these things seriously, just as much as people in America believe in ghosts and demons.

A "Fairy" – from MacRitchie's
Testimony of Tradition

LEPRECHAUNS, TROLLS, GNOMES, AND ELVES

What do these little people represent? According to historians like Massey and MacRitchie, these little beings were originally based on little Black people. Not Black people again! Yes, Black people.

That is, the different traditions of leprechauns, trolls, gnomes, elves, fairies, fians, picts, pixies, and other "wee folk" myths were originally based on the indigenous people of Europe. Some were tall like the "giants" described above, but many resembled the short-statured Black people known throughout the world as pygmies and Negritos.

These Black people were typically descendants of the first African populations to settle the world. For a variety of reasons we explore in *When the World was Black, Part One*, they looked just like taller Black populations, but thousands of years of isolation had made them much smaller than their more recent neighbors.

As we explain elsewhere in that book, these DBP (or Dimunitive Black People) were either feared or highly revered wherever they were encountered. Some were believed to have magic powers, and their "semi-divine" status soon gave way to an almost entirely legendary status. By the time the DBP were rarely seen in those areas, they'd become the subject of myth and embellishment, eventually giving way to legends of "fairies" and other small magical beings. In several of David MacRitchie's works, he traces such beings back to their Black roots.

In Helene Guerber's *Myths of Northern Lands*, we learned that they were called "black dwarves" and "dark elves" not because of symbolism, but because of their "swarthy complexions." Guerber continues:

> These small beings were so homely, with their dark skin, green eyes, large heads, short legs, and crow's feet, that they were told to hide underground and never show themselves during the daytime under penalty of being turned into stone. Although less powerful than the gods, they were far more intelligent than men, and as their knowledge was boundless and extended even to the future, gods and men were equally anxious to question them.

The idea that these "wee people" could "sprite" away and disappear into the crevices of trees may have referred to their retreats into the dense forests. If it was said that they could slip into the cracks of rocks, this may have referred to them eluding potential captors by hiding in caverns and underground dwellings that seemed otherwise uninhabitable. Guerber adds:

> They were also known as trolls, kobolds, brownies, goblins, pucks, or Huldra folk, according to the country where they dwelt. These dwarfs could transport themselves with marvelous celerity [speed] from one place to another, loved to conceal themselves behind rocks, and mischievously repeated the last words of every conversation they overheard. Owing to this well-known trick, the echoes were called dwarfs' talk, and people fancied that the reason

why they were never seen was because each dwarf was the proud possessor of a tiny red cap which made the wearer invisible.[156]

Such embellished stories, like the tales of *Mo-le* in China, were based on the DBP's very real desire to avoid the new populations who threatened their existence. After several thousand years of such encounters, the DBP were quite good at eluding others in this way.

AFRICANS UNDERGROUND

In many cases, the little Black people we call DBP were said to live underground. Robert Halliburton, author of *How a Race of Pygmies was Found in North Africa and Spain*, writes:

> In northern Morocco there is a belief that there is under the ground a race of little men who can be heard at work. Two centuries ago it was said that this belief existed also in Wales...A reference to Mr. MacRitchie's interesting little work, *The Testimony of Tradition* shows that the memory of a dwarf race of smiths was once reverenced by the Irish...

> We need not regard with incredulity [doubt], or "with a disdainful smile," **the veneration of the Moors and of the Monbuttoo for these dwarfs, for the very same superstition still exists among some of our peasantry,** though it is now between one and two thousand years, at least, since the dwarf race in Britain died out, and was represented by "the Little People," that haunt the fairy "knowes" or mounds of Wales and Ireland.

> If any practical joker were to visit (after due notice of his coming and its professed object), all the "fairy mounds" in secluded districts in Wales and Ireland, and were to pretend to go through a form of exorcising and banishing "the Good People" from their ancient homes, **he would create a storm among the peasantry that would rather astonish him.**

Compare these words with what we've already said about how strongly Europeans feel about their Black images of Christ and the Madonna. These were powerful traditions, not to be toyed with.

BLACK CYCLOPS AND THE ALL-SEEING EYE

These little Black people, as we find regarding Black gods nearly everywhere they were worshipped, were masters of their crafts. They were shamans, scientists, and healers of great renown:

> In Europe and Britain the dwarfs of early ages are remembered as smiths, artificers and magicians, but no one has conjectured where they can have come from...The little and the larger Haratin are still great workers in metal, magicians and potent doctors...

He says these little Haratin – a name given to a class of indigenous people in the Sahara – must have "astonished the natives" wherever they went because they wore a *haik* (like a cape) with "a large eye on its back." "It is probable," he says, "that the earliest traditions of Greece described wandering bands of masons and smiths as "the men with the eye," which in time may have become "the men with only one eye" – the Cyclopes."

Halliburton connects these people to the Garamantes of North Africa, who dug the famous system of wells and underground aqueducts that brought water and life back to the Sahara Desert:

> The skill of the modern Cyclops is devoted to sinking deep wells. The well-sinkers of Morocco come from the Dra to the cities north of the Atlas, and are still to be seen wearing their Cyclopean haik.

He notes that this "all-seeing eye" may have been the origin of the Masonic symbol. Thus, not only did the DBP give birth to the Greek legends of the Cyclops, but also to the symbol of the all-seeing eye.

THE SEVEN DWARVES WERE BLACK?

According to Halliburton, these little Black people were even the source material for the fairytale of Snow White and the Seven Dwarves! In fact, he says, the Seven Dwarves didn't simply represent a group of DBP, but a pantheon of the seven oldest gods:

> [T]he father of the gods, the oldest of all, Vulcan or Patah, the eighth of the earliest system of Egyptian deities…was represented as a dwarf. Classical mythology has made Vulcan lame and deformed, while his workmen, "the seven Cyclopes," were supposed to represent the earliest race of men, those progenitors of mankind whom the Hindoos worship as the Pitris [ancestor gods].
>
> If he, the greatest, was a dwarf, the other seven must also have been dwarfs. What a beginning for the gods of antiquity – seven dwarf masons with their pygmy mastermason! Well may the Haratin boast, as their ancestors, the old Atlantes, did, that they are the oldest people in the world, and that all other nations got their gods from them…

Halliburton says this original pantheon of seven Black gods was to be found in Egypt, Palestine, Syria, Phoenicia, India, Rome, and later throughout all of Europe:

> Nor was this earliest form of the Godhead, the deification of pygmies, confined to Egypt, for Selden says that all the greatest gods of Palestine and Syria were Pataeki [pygmy gods], and he shows that little images of them were supposed to bring safety and good luck, and were placed on prows of ships by the Phoenicians…
>
> Probably in Rome they were the venerated Penates, who were classed among the Cabeiri [a group of mysterious "underworld"

gods], and were household gods, which, under different names, were worshipped among so many nations of antiquity. It was, perhaps, a feeling that it was unlucky to speak of these pygmy deities that has thrown a cloud of mystery over the Cabiric divinities of antiquity.

Little Black People in Moorish Spain?

We still haven't addressed the question of where these Black people came from. First, I want to cite one more place where they could be found. Would you believe that these little Black people were to be found in Moorish Spain? And would you believe that even the Moors themselves considered them to be the holiest and purest people around? Don't worry, I've got good sources.

As he notes in great detail in his groundbreaking work on the little Black people of North Africa and Spain, the Moors of North Africa told Halliburton that these "pygmies" were "very holy men" of unknown religion. Some said they were "idolaters" and "worship Didoo Osiri" (or "Osuru"). This god may have some connection to Ausar (Osiris).

Otherwise, they were the object of great secrecy. "Why do so many of the Moors dread strangers knowing about this pygmy race?" he asks. Halliburton continues:

> Sometimes I had little difficulty in getting the Moors to speak of them, though they have exclaimed with surprise, "How do you come to know anything about them?" But superstitious natives, and especially the Haratin living near Tamanart in the Dra Valley, have often cut short the conversation on my pressing them to tell me as to the numbers and place of residence of the dwarfs, etc. One said, "It is a sin to speak about them to you. I shall say nothing." Others say, "God has sent them to us. We must not talk about them."

> A young Jew now living in Manchester, but a native of Mogador, said that **the Moors worshipped these Barakers** [a name for the DBP], and would not talk freely about them to the Jews. He had tried to find out about them, but without success. He had constantly, when a boy, seen an old Baraker who died at Mogador about eight or ten, years ago, who was looked on as a great saint, and as such was kissed on the shoulders by the Moors as they passed him in the street.

> These dwarfs are supposed to bring good luck to the towns where they reside, and are guardians and protectors, resembling in this respect the Palladium of the Trojans. **If strangers were to succeed in carrying them out of the country, good luck would depart with them.**

Halliburton notes that this nearly fanatic devotion to these Black people was similar to the devotion shown to Akka pygmies in Central Africa:

> The Monbuttoo regard the Akkas "as a sort of benevolent spirits or mandrakes, who are in no way detrimental."…It is probable that some such superstitious belief was at the bottom of the difficulty which puzzled and baffled Schweinfurth in his attempt to get a sight of the dwarf Akkas of the Monbutto country, the king of which sent away by night his regiment of dwarfs, so as to keep them out of the way of his visitor.

So where did these little holy men come from? In his book, Halliburton credits David MacRitchie for his contributions to the study of the DBP in Europe, but contends that they were not, as MacRitchie suggested, extinct everywhere:

> Writers on the Isle of Man and the Highlands seem to agree that the fairies represent an extinct dwarf race. Mr. MacRitchie seeks for existing representatives of it among the Eskimo, Laplanders, and even the distant Ainos. It is possible that we may find some survivals of this race of dwarfs without going as far north as the Arctic regions, or as far south as the Albert Nyanza or the Congo.[157]

In other words, the famed "dwarf race," who gave birth to the European belief in fairies and other magical beings, was not extinct, nor were its only survivors to be found in distant outposts of Asia and the Arctic. Instead, Halliburton wrote, their kin could still be found in Inner Africa. Halliburton connects the Akka in the Southern Atlas Mountains of North Africa to the pygmies of "Equatorial Akka" in Central Africa.

As British Egyptologist Gerald Massey explains, any European myth involving a "little person" is likely leftover "debris" from African DBP history.

> Africa, the home of the pygmies, is presumably the birthplace of the dwarf races now represented by the diminutive wee folk of the Dark Continent. The earliest emigrants who made their way out of that land and wandered over Europe would be akin to these in stature, like the Lapps who follow them at a short distance. These were the wee folk in human form.
>
> But there is another factor to be taken into account before we can ascertain the origin of the wee folk as spirits in a tiny fairy shape. These do not simply represent the pygmy race of human beings, but are the same primitive people translated into spirit-world, from the time when the race was of the pygmy stature.
>
> We gather from the secret wisdom that the earliest beings who entered the nether earth were dwarfs or dwarfish people. The god Ptah, who opened the under-world by tunneling the mount of Amenta, is himself a dwarf. The seven khnemmu that assisted him

were pygmies.

First come the African pygmies. Second, the mythical pygmies of Ptah. Third, the human souls that are the same in stature. Fourth, the wee folk of the legends, who inhabit the mounds, who work the mines, who dwell beneath the sea, the natural, the mythical, and spiritualistic dwarfs being somewhat mixed up together.

The marchen or folk-tales of the Asiatic and European races are the debris of Egyptian mythos. Fairyland is no conception of the Kelt [Celt], nor original product of the Aryan imagination; it is the Kamite earth of eternity in the lower world of the mount of earth which was excavated by the pygmies of the opener Ptah.

From no other land or literature than the Egyptian can we explain the wee folk in the [European] fairy mound [which is called the] Sfd. (pronounced shee, coming from the Egyptian she or shu, for the hollow, the void, and sheta, the sarcophagus.)[158]

SURTR, A BLACK NORSE GOD?

In 2010, white supremacists went nuts because the producers of the film *Thor* had decided to cast Idris Elba, a Black man, as one of the Norse gods. You may not know this, but white supremacists are nearly fanatic about Norse mythology, because Nordic people (who are seen as the "purest" white Europeans) celebrated their conquest of others in their mythology.

Much of it is pure carnage, with tales of bloodshed and brutality everywhere, often involving white gods destroying those who are presumably not white. There is even an "end of the world" scenario known as Ragnarok, which white supremacists associate with a race war that will end all race wars. Considering all this, it does seem silly to cast a Black man as a Nordic god. But would anyone believe that there were, indeed, Black gods among the Norse?

Surtr is one of the jotunn of Norse mythology. He was a Black giant with a flaming sword. In Old Norse, his name literally means "black" or "the swarthy one." According to the *Prose Edda*, he is stationed at the frontiers of the impassible mountain realm, Múspellheim, the "land of fire," where he prevents anyone from crossing. Nobody knows where Múspellheim is, but it is definitely a southern land, and may have been the Caucasus.

It is believed that Surtr would lead others who guarded the region, known as "Múspell's sons," on horseback to Ragnarök, where – after a long battle – they would defeat Freyr (a Norse high god), and "set fire to the world" and the other Norse gods.

In the Norse epic *Gylfaginning*, it is written:

Surtr travels from the south with the stick-destroyer (fire). Shines from his sword the sun of the gods of the slain. Rock cliffs crash and troll-wives are abroad, heroes tread the road of Hel and heaven splits...Amid this turmoil the sky will open and from it will ride the sons of Muspell. Surtr will ride in front, and both before and behind him there will be burning fire. His sword will be splendid. Light will shine from it more brightly than from the sun.

Modern rendition of Norse God Surtr

Is this story somehow connected to the cherubs with flaming swords who guard the gates after God drives Adam and Eve out of the Garden of Eden? Was Fard Muhammad right about the armed Black sentinels who kept whites in the Caucasus? We'll revisit Surtr and the story of his origins in Volume Four of *The Science of Self*.

Crom Dubh

CROM DUBH

Crom Dubh (the "Black Crom") was a Celtic god of fertility. It is believed he was represented by the stone pillars that were erected throughout Ireland during prehistoric times. In later times, this Black god came to be considered an "evil" god as Christianity spread through Europe and all "pagan" deities, especially the Black ones, were suppressed and associated with the devil. According to legend, St. Patrick overcame Black Crom to establish Christianity across Ireland, a feat still recognized today on Crom Dubh Sunday.

WHO IS BAPHOMET?

Ever heard of Baphomet? Demon god of the Illuminati, right? Not really. I almost left this section out of the book. There are so many misguided and misinformed theories that surround the "secret" teachings of the Freemasons and other fraternal organizations that I thought it would be better to dedicate an entire book to making sense of these matters. And the other part of me just didn't want to engage this stuff. I mean, people really have their facts wrong. Part of the problem is the sources we consult for our information nowadays. Too many of us are consulting YouTube scholars and cuckoo authors, failing to properly research the information for ourselves.

At the last minute, I decided to add a little commentary on the infamous Baphomet. Baphomet, if you didn't know, is also known as a "Black God," but mostly in the sense that he is thought of as a "dark spirit" or demon, sometimes called the Black Goat. The way the story goes, Baphomet was a demon worshipped by the Knights Templar, who are considered the predecessors of the Freemasons.

Since people don't know any of the distinctions between any of these groups, they call them all Illuminati. Since before the time of the Knights Templar, the Catholic Church was teaching that any belief not approved by the Church was heretic, pagan, and downright *of the devil.* Thus, Baphomet is supposed to be Satan, and the Illuminati (or all the groups that can be called that) worship this evil Baphomet.

What's the real story? The real story, based on the historical evidence that we have today, is that the Knights Templar, an elite Christian order, were indeed persecuted by King Philip IV of France in the early 1300s. But this was because they had begun adopting Islamic practices from the Moors. In fact, the whole Western institution of banking and checking comes from this cultural transfer. At some point, the Church wasn't pleased, and began suspecting the Knights Templar of worshipping non-Christian gods. So, naturally, they started imprisoning and torturing them.

Nobody told, at least, nobody told anything useful. They said crazy things, but none of them said the same thing as another. Yet somehow, they arrived at a name, Baphomet. Nobody could say what

Baphomet looked like, but some accounts said the Knights worshipped either "a human skull, a stuffed human head, or a metal or wooden human head with curly black hair." But no goat.

It wasn't until 1856, when French magician Eliphas Levi illustrated "The Baphomet of Mendes," based on a mix of the Tarot card for the Devil and images of Banebdjedet, a goat-headed god worshipped in Mendes, ancient Egypt.[159] Right, Levi made it up. And he made a ton of money doing so. Then, in the 1960s, the Church of Satan adopted this image, added the upside-down

Eliphas Levi's "Black Goat"

pentagram, and then trademarked it. They made a ton of money as well. People tend to get excited about this kinda stuff, you see. And they don't care if it's real, so long as it seems interesting and creepy.

So where's the name Baphomet come from? It definitely goes back to the time of the Knights Templar, but most historians agree that it's simply a French corruption of the name Muhammad (from Mahomet).[160]

But would the Knights Templar, a group having some extensive esoteric knowledge, simply worship the Prophet Muhammad? If so, why a wooden head with "curly black hair"? And why were they so concerned with protecting this secret that they would accept torture and death before telling of their true god? In 1865, Thomas Wright reported that Knights would kiss the feet of painted wooden idols who represented Baphomet, and that these practices were somehow tied to the Saracens, or Moors. He adds:

Egyptian God Banebdjedet

> A templar of Florence declared that, in the secret chapters of the order, one brother said to the other, showing the idol, "Adore this head—this head is your god and your Mahomet."[161]

In other words, the Knights Templar had definitely learned something from the Moors, but it wasn't traditional Islam. Even in 1865, Knight wasn't convinced that "Mahomet" didn't actually represent something else more secretive.

We know that the god of the Knights Templar (and perhaps the many secret societies who descended from them) was not a goat-man, nor was he Satan. In order to understand who these men may have really worshipped in private, you'll have to keep reading.

THE POPE AND HIS GOD

As far north as Ireland, there are early Celtic crosses inscribed with the *bismillah* ("In the Name of Allah", the opening words of the Qur'an) written in kufic Arabic. Why?

Meanwhile, there are devotional images depicting Black-skinned Moors throughout Europe, even in places where we don't have much evidence of Moorish occupation. These images are often found alongside depictions of a Black Madonna and Christ. Religious historians ignore these icons, but they are most definitely there. Many are still available in the public view.

THE CHAIR OF ST. PETER

Other pieces of evidence might be harder to find. The Chair of St. Peter, the *Cathedra Petri*, is such an item. This is the chair where Popes would sit to pass down dogmas for the entire Catholic Church. It dates back to around 875 AD, but is considered so holy that it was once regarded as the chair of St. Peter himself. It isn't however, the most visible part of the Vatican's collection.

Why not? I'll explain. In 1798, when the French took over Rome during the French Revolution, some of the French soldiers wanted to "investigate" the relics stored in the Vatican. This is when they found St. Peter's Chair. Under a layer of dust and cobwebs, they discovered that the back of this chair held an unexpected surprise: an inscription in Arabic characters – the well-known confession of Islamic faith, 'There is no God but Allah, and Mohammed is his prophet.'

Think about it. This is a holy chair. *Of the Pope.* The Pope! And it's saying what?

Naturally, things nearly went nuts. But the folks in power managed to keep this discovery relatively quiet. In 1851, a writer named Lady Morgan proposed a way to resolve the confusion: let the chair be examined by a group of experts chosen from Catholic and Protestant scholars. Yet the chair was never closely investigated.

THE POPE AND THE BLACK MADONNA

If you Google the Black Madonna, you'll find countless images of Popes – both past and present – kneeling at her feet, bowing before her, or kissing her hand. If the Black Christ is with her, it's even more serious. There's some sort of reverence for the Black Mary and Christ that you won't find for other images and icons. But why?

A rare meeting between Popes. What did they discuss?

Is this a Christian convention – to venerate Black images more than others? Earlier, we learned that these icons were especially sacred because of the older, pre-Christian traditions they were connected to. So what does it mean that we see the esteemed leaders of the Church prostrating themselves before symbols that have been connected to pre-European "paganism"? Some critics say these gestures of worship for Black deities hint at Satanism, but we also have learned that the "black" image of Satan was based on an actual Black god, not the idea of evil. So who are these guys worshipping?

THE POPE WHO QUIT

Fast forward to the reign of Pope Benedict XVI (Joseph Ratzinger, 2005–2013). You know, the guy who actually QUIT being Pope. Yeah, that's not common. This marks the first time a pope has resigned in nearly 600 years. He basically said he wasn't with the program anymore. By "program" I mean that thing they do where they just shuffle the pedophile priests around from one district to another, rather than kicking them out for good.

In 2009, Pope Benedict sat down with Muslim leaders and Voldoun

(Voodoo) priests in West Africa (yes!), where he talked about the *source* of the crises affecting Africa:

> Without discussing the genesis of such sickness of the spirit, it is nevertheless indisputable that the so-called 'first' world has sometimes exported and is exporting toxic spiritual refuse which contaminates the peoples of other continents, including in particular the population of Africa.

In other words, the white people in power have screwed up the world, especially Africa. Rather than attempt to continue the old program, or to work overtime restoring the reputation of the Church (as he'd been expected to do), Pope Benedict said he only wanted to answer to the Will of God. But who is his God?

THE PAPAL COAT OF ARMS

Every Pope has a Papal Coat of Arms, which acts as a symbol of his Papacy. Pope Benedict became the first Pope to feature the face of a person on his coat of arms. The face? A Moor, prominently featured in the top left corner of the emblem. His skin is black, his features are African, and unlike many of the Moors depicted in old European imagery, he doesn't wear a cloth on his head. He wears a crown.

When pressed about this image, he played dumb. "I do not know its meaning" he said. Yeah right. Just as I'm sure the Popes who sat in (and later hid) St. Peter's Chair had no idea what was written on it.

WHAT'S REALLY GOING ON?

This should lead you to wonder, who do they really worship? What else are they hiding in the Vatican? What did Pope Benedict know? Why did he leave the Papacy? We know he resigned after receiving the results of an internal investigation, citing what one journalist listed as "blackmail, corruption and gay sex at the Vatican." But was there more to the story? Not long before he left, he did something else no other Pope had done before (publicly, at least). In front of 20,000 pilgrims on St Peter's Square, he prayed in Arabic.

We know there are countless images of Popes praying to Black icons. But is there more to the story? Is there a connection between the Pope and a "secret Islamic tradition"? Is the Black man on Benedict's coat of arms, being both a symbol for Islam and royalty, a symbol for something – or *someone* – even bigger? Who do they *really* pray to?

Papal Coat of Arms of Pope Benedict

THE GODS OF THE AMERICAS

FROM THE OLMECS TO THE INUIT

> *"Several Indian nations, such as the Mayans, Aztecs, and Incas, worshipped black gods along with their other deities, and the Mayan religion particularly exemplifies the high esteem in which the negroes were held."* – Harold G. Lawrence, The Crisis, 1962

Many Native American gods were Black. Runoko Rashidi explains:

> Other scientists have found a host of cultural parallels between ancient Africans and Native Americans, including architectural patterns and religious practices. As for the latter, some Native American communities worshipped black gods of great antiquity, such as Ekchuah, Quetzalcoatl, Yalahau, Nahualpilli and Ixtliltic, long before the first enslaved Africans arrived in the New World.

In this chapter, we'll explore the Black gods of the Americas.

THE BLACK GODS OF MEXICO

THE BLACK CHRIST OF LATIN AMERICA

> *"The missionaries wanted to press the Indigenous people into submission, but the Indigenous people ended up bringing the White God into submission. The God of the Nahuatl triumphed…"*
> *– Armando Lampe, Along the Many Paths of God*

Ever wondered why there are so many images of a Black Christ throughout Latin America? Well, it wasn't always the Spaniards who brought this tradition over from Europe. In many cases, the Black Christ was a mix of Spanish Catholicism and indigenous tradition.

T.W. Doane, author of *Bible Myths,* acknowledges a "Mexican crucified god being sometimes represented as black," and that "crosses were also found in Yucatan, as well as Mexico, with a man upon them." What was odd, however, was that these artifacts were said to predate the presence of Christianity in the region.

As John G. Jackson notes in *Ethiopia and the Origin of Civilization*:

> Mr. A. H. Verrill, an American archaeologist, visited an Indian shrine in a small town in Guatemala a few years ago, and found that on a special festival day Indians traveled to this little church to bow down to the image of a Black Christ. From the attendant ceremonies, Verrill judged the rite to be of Mayan origin.[162]

In other words, there were Black gods revered throughout the area, long before the Europeans came. When the missionaries

Black Christ, Mexico City

began talking about Jesus, some of the indigenous people believed they must have been talking about one of their own Black gods.

Ekchuah

EKCHUAH, THE BLACK STAR

These gods were worshipped far and wide. For example, Ekchuah was the sixth most commonly depicted deity in the Mayan codices, portrayed at least forty times.

He is painted Black with thick lips. **His name means "Black Star"** (*ek* means "star" and *chuah* means "black" in Yucatan Maya).

Floyd Hayes III reports that among many of the Indians of Guatemala, "the black Christ is referred to in private as Ekchuah," who Harold Lawrence describes as "black and woolly-haired" and "unmistakably Negro."

Lawrence adds:

> An examination of ancient Indian religions yields additional information of the condition of early Africans in the Americas. Several Indian nations, such as the Mayans, Aztecs, and Incas, worshipped black gods along with their other deities, and the Mayan religion particularly exemplifies the high esteem in which the negroes were held.[163]

In *Africa and the Discovery of America*, Leo Weiner connects the Mayan god Ekchuah to the African Nama societies of the Malinke and Bambara peoples of West Africa.

Yucatán Postclassic Maya as God "M"

Modern rendering of God M, based on Codex Madrid

GOD M, AN AFRICAN MEDICINE MAN?

Ekchuah may have been based on an older Black god, known to us only as God M. God M is represented throughout the ancient codices as a Black god, specifically an "old man" with a toothless jaw or one tooth. He appears to be a trader, often shown carrying goods on his head.

Images of him suggest that he was also somehow related to bee-keeping. What's so special about bees? Plenty. It's known that the ancient Mexicans kept bees. Their specific breed typically produced irregular honeycombs with cells having three to six sides.

So most of the Mayan manuscripts feature honeycombs having four sides, short of the "perfection" found in the hexagonal (six-sided) honeycombs of Africa. This is why it's important to note, as Schellhas does, that "the black god M" is only shown holding hexagonal honeycombs. These are African honeycombs.

Still not sure why bees are important? In Volume Three of *Africa and the Discovery of America*, Weiner remarks on the significance of the honeybee among the Malinkes and Bambaras of West Africa and their *Nama* societies, noting that their chief medicine was made from honey. Thus their healers lived in huts made to resemble beehives. Weiner says their reverence for the bee can be traced back to the Qur'an, where it is written:

> Thy Lord spake by inspiration unto the bee, saying, Provide thee houses in the mountains and in the trees, and of those materials wherewith men build hives for thee: then eat of every kind of fruit, and walk in the beaten paths of thy Lord. There proceedeth from their bellies a liquor of various colour, wherein is a medicine for men. Verily herein is a sign unto people who consider.

As we explain in *The Hood Health Handbook*, honey is indeed a multi-purpose medicine. It's a natural antibiotic, cough suppressant, and does all kinds of other important stuff. But, beyond its medicinal properties, it appears that the bees themselves are symbolic of something greater, at least for those "who consider."

Weiner says West Africans like the Malinkes and Bambaras made voyages to the Americas long before Columbus. He identifies many of the Mayan and Aztec gods as being derived from the reverence paid to these Black visitors.

As he and several others have noted, the Black gods of the Americas are typically gods of medicine and healing, trade, or music and dance. According to these scholars, these associations are based on the traditions introduced by actual Black people.

Weiner says of the black-faced god Ixtlilton:

> [He was] a dance god, just like a "medicine" *griot*. That he [derived] from the *Nama* worship follows from his use of the "black water," which…refers to a honeyed drink, used as medicine.

Perhaps some of these Black gods were revered for introducing a treasured medicine, made from West African honey?

GOD L, A TRADER AND WARRIOR

In addition to God M, there's also another Black god in the manuscripts, known as God L. Paul Schellhas calls him the "Old Black God." Not much more is known about his significance. As Schellhas explains:

> The significance of god L does not appear from the few pictures, which are given of him. In Dr. 46b the god is pictured armed and in warlike attitude. Both in Dr. 14b and 14c he wears a bird on his head and has a Kan in his hand.[164]

Don't get the wrong idea about the "warrior" character of these gods. They didn't come only to bring war. They came to do trade. But, as Schellhas notes about God M, "the travelling merchant must, of course, be armed to ward off hostile attacks."[165]

God L - Temple of the Cross

God L is also portrayed smoking some the kind of "cigar" often associated with shamans. Many of these Black gods wear headdresses made to look like birds, just as we find among the Black gods of Egypt. At least one of these Black gods is depicted carrying a spear.

In *The Myths of Mexico and Peru*, Lewis Spence says God L may have been related to another Black god of the Americas, Votan, or to the black Aztec god Tepeyollotl.

THE MAYAN PRIESTS

Frederick Peterson, in his 1959 work *Ancient Mexico*, remarked:

We can trace the slow progress of man in Mexico without noting any definite Old World influence during this period (1000-650 BC), except possibly a strong Negroid substratum connected with the Magicians.[166]

The "Magicians" may have been West Africans who traveled to Mexico or a class of Black people who could only marry among themselves, effectively preserving the African phenotype over untold generations. This reverence for Black people may have something to do with why many Native Americans, including the Mayas, respected enslaved Africans and revered Black gods that represented the principles of healing and good fortune.

Later, when the influx of Black people decreased, many Mesoamerican priests began painting themselves Black to continue this tradition, which continues today. But it didn't begin with black body paint. It began with black skin. Although Fred Peterson later denied his claims about a Black presence in Mexico, there's now plenty of evidence to prove it.

In Part Two of *When the World was Black,* we devote several pages to the Black priests and shamans depicted by the Mayans in the Bonampak and Xultun murals. Regarding a little-known mural in Guatemala that has almost entirely been ignored by mainstream research, I write:

> And then I found out more. The photographers were intentionally leaving out three figures seated behind the scribe! Why? Because they REALLY looked African. In fact, they're painted nearly jet black, and are wearing what archaeologist William Saturno calls "headdresses of a sort never before seen in Maya art." When you see the picture of these headdresses, it's obvious what they look like. The crowns of Egyptian pharaohs.
>
> Could these Black men – hidden from most media reports on the site – be remnants of a Nubian expedition that landed in Central America? Are these "three wise men" from the East? Or did they descend from the Olmec? And – considering that the scribe is making calculations for the Mayan calendar – what exactly is the role of these seated, crowned, observers?[167]

If these three were, indeed, travelers who came from the east, establishing themselves as men who were qualified to supervise the calculations of the Mayan calendar, would they not have been seen as living gods? Would they later become revered as gods like Ekchuah?

There's more to this mural. I continue:

> And there's yet another hidden figure, this one hidden by the artists themselves! "Older Brother Obsidian," who may be a king, has more of the classic Native American features, and is a shade of lighter brown, looking like many Mayas today. But behind him, a dark-skinned male is seated, mostly concealed by the throne. It looks like a scene from the Wizard of Oz, with the man in the back manipulating the arms of the figure in the front.
>
> If that weren't enough, a rod above this part of the mural was once used to hang a curtain, which could conceal or reveal the dark-skinned man behind the throne. What does all of this mean? What does it prove? And what more lays hidden? According to Saturno, although the Xultun site was first discovered in 1915, less than 0.1 percent of it has been explored.[168]

Unless one of us makes it our business to dig deeper, I'd venture to say that this site won't be revisited much…for obvious reasons.

TEZCATLIPOCA, THE AZTEC GOD

Tezcatlipoca was one of the most important gods in ancient Mesoamerica. He began as important deity for the Toltecs and later became the supreme god of the Aztecs. He was seen as a Creator, the god of sustenance, a patron god of warriors, and the bringer of both good and evil. Like other gods associated with destruction, he maintained change and renewal through conflict.

As a multifaceted deity, he appears in many incarnations. Of these, the one known as "Black Tezcatlipoca" is the most feared and highly revered. Few artistic representations of him have survived, but the earliest ones represent him as black. His priests would cover themselves in black soot or charcoal to associate themselves

Mosaic Skull Mask of Tezcatlipoca

with the Black god. They would also paint the newly appointed king black to associate him with Tezcatlipoca.[169]

The worship of Tezcatlipoca goes back to the earliest Mesoamerican deities worshipped by the Olmec and Maya. Scholars have connected him to the patron god the Mayan *Popol Vuh*, the god Tohil, whose name means "obsidian" (a black stone).[170]

OPOCHTLI

Opochtli (meaning "The Left-Handed") was an Aztec god sacred to fishermen and bird-catchers. At one time, the ancestors of the Aztecs relied heavily on fishing and bird-catching for their survival.

Opochtli is credited with the invention or introduction of the fishing net, the bird net, and the harpoon. According

Opochtli

to Lewis Spence, "He was represented as a man painted black, his head decorated with the plumes of native wild birds, and crowned by a paper coronet in the shape of a rose."[171]

THE BLACK LORD AND OTHERS

There are many other Black gods who were recognized across ancient Mexico. Paul Schelhas notes a number of black figures in the *Codex Troano* who are different from gods L and M. He notes another Black god in the Paris manuscript, and cites yet another in the Tzendals manuscript (in addition to Ekchuah), who is called Xicalahua, or "black lord."[172]

In *Myths of Mexico and Peru*, Spence notes a Black god known across Mexico by many names, including Tata (or "Our Father"), Huehueteotl ("Oldest of the Gods"), and Xiuhteculi ("Lord of the Year").[173] He had a black face, and wore a headdress of green feathers and a golden serpent on his back. At one time, all families made offerings to this god after a child was born.

THE OLMEC GODS

We can't talk about ancient Mesoamerica without talking about the Olmecs. We've already talked about how cultural leaders can easily become revered as gods, especially after they've "disappeared." We'll revisit that idea here.

When people think about the Olmec civilization, they often wonder, "Who were the men represented in those colossal stone heads?" Were they leaders? Warriors? Traders? Gods? As we explain in *When the World Was Black*, the evidence suggests that it was all of the above:

> Around 3000 BC, an influx of people arrived along the western shores of the Americas. They most likely sailed from East Asia, after island-hopping across the Pacific Ocean via a current known as the Kuro-shiwa, or "Black Stream." The name is fitting, as it seems many of these migrants were Black people who had settled in East Asia. When these people arrived, maize cultivation suddenly became advanced, and spreads far and wide, reaching the Andes by 2500 BC, and the indigenous people of the American southwest by 2100 BC.[174] It was probably the Black Mokaya people of the Pacific Coast of Mexico who introduced maize to the Olmec heartland, where it quickly became the staple crop of the Olmec, with some gods clearly being associated with maize production. In fact, the maize fields are where the Olmec farmers placed their colossal stone heads, suggesting that the people represented by these heads may have had something to do with its cultivation.

BLACK GODS IN THE AMERICAN SOUTHEAST

THE OLD MAN VERSUS THE GREAT SPIRIT

Often, when we hear about the beliefs of North American Indians, we hear of a "Great Spirit" that no one can see or describe. This is, however, not as authentic as you might think. Most of the deities who were indigenous to the Americas were characterized as living beings. In some cases, the forces of nature were personified as people (or animals), but in many cases, there were real people at the roots of these traditions.

The original "high God" of many North American cosmologies was described as an "Old Man." He may have been a patriarch or ancestral character, or he may have been a cultural leader. Whatever the case, he was described as a flesh-and-blood man, and Christian missionaries were threatened by this idea.

Thus they introduced the idea of a "Great Spirit." They used the term "Great Spirit" as often as they could, even in describing Native

American beliefs, in an attempt to replace the older, "primitive" with one of their own. As a result, many Native American oral traditions record some sort of competition between this Great Spirit and the Old Man (or some other human figure). Ethnographers Wissler and Duvall report:

> There was once a Great Spirit who was good. He made a man and a woman. Then Old Man came along. No one made Old Man; he always existed.

This suggests that the "Old Man" tradition predates the "Great Spirit" that may have been introduced by Christian missionaries.

> The Great Spirit said to him, "Old Man, have you any power?" "Yes," said Old Man, "I am very strong." "Well," said the Great Spirit, "suppose you make some mountains." So Old Man set to work and made the Sweet-Grass Hills. To do this he took a piece of Chief Mountain. He brought Chief Mountain up to its present location, shaped it up, and named it. The other mountains were called blood colts.

This seems to represent the practice of mound-building, which we'll discuss later.

> "Well," said the Great Spirit, "you are strong." "Now," said Old Man, "there are four of us, — the man and woman, you and I." The Great Spirit said, "All right."

Contrary to ideas that the Great Spirit was seen as the God that was above all, here we see this Great Spirit as simply another mythical personality.

> The Great Spirit said, "I will make a big cross for you to carry." Old Man said "No, you make another man so that he can carry it." The Great Spirit made another man. Old Man carried the cross a while, but soon got tired and wanted to go. The Great Spirit told him that he could go, but he should go out among the people and the animals, and teach them how to live, etc.
>
> Now the other man got tired of carrying the cross. He was a white man. The Great Spirit sent him off as a traveller. So he wandered on alone. [175]

Here the Christian missionary influence becomes clear. Yet there is also clear resistance, with the Blackfoot symbolically rejecting the white man and his white Jesus as cultural leaders, instead portraying them as wanderers. The cross motif isn't indigenous, so it only occurs as a representation of Christian influence.

However, if there's any significance to the Old Man having first carried the cross, it could stem from missionaries telling the Blackfoot about the Crucifixion narrative, where Simon of Cyrene, a Black man, carries the cross for a while before Jesus.[176]

If nothing else, we can see that the gods of Native American communities – including the most important deities – were not seen as "only" spirit, but were also regarded as living, breathing, humans.

THE "OLD MAN" LEADS AND TEACHES

In a Blackfoot myth describing their migration to Canada and the Great Plains, they appear to remember their ancestors' journey across the Bering Strait:

> The first Indians were on the other side of the ocean, and Old Man decided to lead them to a better place. So he brought them over the ice to the far north.[177]

Among the Tsuu T'ina Nation of Canada, there is a myth recalling the same migration. Both myths note that somewhere in the Canada, possibly near Alberta, their ancestors were split into two groups. In the Blackfoot version, the frozen ground split, forcing the people to separate.[178]

Wissler and Duval continue the Blackfoot myth as follows:

> Now Old Man led these people down to where the Blood Reserve now is, and told them that this would be a fine country for them, and that they would be very rich. He said, "I will get all the people here." All the people living there ate and lived like wild animals; but Old Man went among them and taught them all the arts of civilization. When he was through teaching them, he did not die, but went among the Sioux, where he remained for a time, but finally disappeared. He took his wife with him. He had no children.[179]

Here, the "Old Man" is a teacher of civilization. But who was he? Was he one of "escorts" proposed in Part One of *When the World was Black*? Or was he simply an ancestral figure?

Throughout Native American tradition, whether Blackfoot or Iroquois, the "Old Man" or "stranger" is the one who introduces the innovations associated with the Anu Cultural Complex (farming, home construction, and other "arts of civilization"). Rarely is he described as "one of the people." He is different. But who does he represent?

THE FALSE FACE SOCIETY OF THE IROQUOIS

In some myths, this "stranger" reveals himself to have supernatural knowledge. In another, the stranger challenges the High God to a contest of power, involving who could move a mountain the farthest. The stranger is amazingly able to move a mountain, but is no match for the Creator, who moves it so close to the stranger that

> **DID YOU KNOW?**
> Iroquois lore speaks of semi-divine 'Stone Giants' who lived in the woods and had 'rock-hard' skin obtained by rolling in earth and sand regularly.
> To this day, Nubian wrestlers cover themselves in ash or white clay, and the Greek legend of Hercules tells of him wrestling an African named Antaeus who draws his power from being connected to the earth.

he disfigures his nose when he turns to see it.* This is said to be the origin of mask – with its twisted face – which the Iroquois' False Face Society uses to honor the stranger.

If you look at ANY of these false face masks, you will see exactly who this stranger was. Might not be a pleasant depiction, but they were saying the stranger was Black. These masks are typically painted black, with the grotesque exaggeration of Black features that you can find in early European and Asian representations of legendary African people (not to mention in some indigenous art as well!). The eyes are large and bright, painted either white or yellow. We find yellow eyes and the same grotesque exaggeration of features in depictions of the Hopi god Chaikwana, who was based on a Black man.

On most masks you can find today, the hair is long and flaxen, made from black, red, or blonde horsehair.

A "False Face" Mask

But before the introduction of horses by the Europeans, they used corn husks and buffalo hair. If you remember Bob Marley's song "Buffalo Soldier" then you know the texture of buffalo hair. Let's just say it's not like horsehair. In fact, among some Native American people, such as the Apache, the word for "Black man," *lizhena*, means "buffalo-black-haired."[180]

It is my theory that the "Old Man" or "stranger" represents one (or a group) of the Anu migrants who we know – based on genetic research – came among many of the indigenous people of the Americas long before Columbus. They were Black people.

---

* In this myth, the Creator God, seeing the stranger's powers, doesn't want him to stay. But the stranger convinces him, on the premise that he would stick around to protect the people and heal them when they called on him. The stranger is sometimes called Grandfather, sometimes Chief.

THE BLACK SHAMANS OF NORTHWEST CANADA

The Iroquois are not the only ones to use masks to commemorate Black people. Across the Americas, we find such masks and carvings. Among the Navajo, such a mask is used to represent the Black God Hastsezini. Even as far north as the Haida of northwest Canada, some of the masks worn by the oldest shamans are made to look just like African or Australian faces.

Haida Shamans

In his *Haida Texts and Myths*, Dr. John Swanton, of the Bureau of American Ethnology, retells a Haida story of young man who visits a house where shamans gathered. In front of the house stood two shamans "with big bellies and black skins." In another story, a young man's uncle asks him about a journey he took recently to the top of a mountain. He says:

> Did you see the one standing there with a black skin? He shoots down on those people below who treat each other badly. Then the land below is also full of smoke, and there is sickness every where...Be watchful. If one always watches, he, too, will live here. **The black man always keeps watch on those who are foolish.**[181]

Was this symbolic? Perhaps we could assume that the Haida had never seen a real Black man before. But this is not true. The Haida knew exactly what a Black man looked like. In fact, in 1912, Swanton reported that "the richest man among the Skidegate Haida is a Negro."[182]

EEYEEKALDUK, A DANGEROUS HEALER

If you thought Northwest Canada seemed like a distant place to find traces of Black men worshipped as gods, you might be surprised to know that we can go even further. Among the Inuit people of Greenland, Canada, and Alaska, Eeyeekalduk is a god of healing. He is described as an old Black man who is so small he lives inside a stone. He is invoked as a miraculous healer of the sick. It is said to be dangerous to look directly into his jet-black face, because – although he could cure one's illness merely by looking into their eyes – he could also give one illness in the same way.

THE MOUNDBUILDERS AND THE WANDERING GODS

Throughout the eastern United States, there are thousands of sites where Indian communities built massive mounds and walls from the earth. In *When the World was Black*, I propose the following theory for their origin:

> In many of these places, a small group of Anu migrants was able to mobilize a large community of people (often a non-agricultural people) to produce these massive monuments. Considering that so many of these mounds (as well as other structures made from stone) were burial sites, it's possible that Anu "teachers" introduced new advances in agriculture, astronomy, urbanization, and social structure – all developments that occur wherever we find these monuments – and the indigenous populations honored them with elaborate burials. These burial sites, fittingly, became astronomical observatories that made full use of the innovations their owners introduced.
>
> Thus it makes sense that – in the tradition of the Lacandón Indians of western Mexico (who descend from the Maya) – it was "unthinkable" to harvest anywhere such mounds existed, as these mounds were believed to be the dwelling place of the Wayantekob, or the "Wandering Gods."[183]

The Moundbuilders may have indeed been "wandering gods," who had come from distant lands to introduce new ways to build communities and civilizations. Such individuals may have been venerated with statues (like the colossal Olmec heads), in shamanic masks (like those of the False Face Society) or in tradition (as in the myths of the "stranger").

THE FIRST YUCHI INDIANS WERE BLACK

In the cosmology of the Yuchi Indians of Tennessee, the Sun and Moon were of the highest rank. Some people were considered to be classed above everyday Yuchi people because they were descended from the Sun himself. In his *Ethnology of the Yuchi Indians*, Frank Gouldsmith Speck notes:

> It should be mentioned here that at certain times since the origin there have been born individuals with a very dark shade of skin. These blackskinned Yuchi, as they are termed, are looked upon as being more closely related to Sun than the rest of the people. They are said to be his direct offspring, their mothers having become pregnant by Sun. As no particular rank is given them, however, their position is a sort of empty aristocracy. Several blackskinned Yuchi are said to be living today, but I have not been fortunate enough to see them.[184]

Speck then gives us the myth that describes these Black Indians who are closest to God:

> There was a Sun and there was a Moon. Then the Moon was in her menstrual courses. When she got up, a drop of the blood fell from her and descended to the earth. The Sun saw it. He secured it and wrapped it up, laying it away thus for four days. On the fourth day he went and got it, and unwrapped it. When the bundle was opened, he saw that it had turned into a human being. Then he said:
>
> "You are my son. You shall be called Tsoyahd." And he gave him the name Tsoyahd, Sun people or Offspring of the Sun. From him all the Yuchi had their origin.
>
> Now his descendants increased until they became a powerful people. **They are weakening now, but if they ever disappear from the earth a terrible thing will happen.** For the Sun said:
>
> "If the Yuchi perish, I will not face this world. I will turn my face away, and there will be darkness upon the earth, and it will even be the last of the earth."
>
> So it will come to pass if all the Yuchi die out. But now there are certain Yuchi who are known to be sons of this Sun. Whenever one of them dies the Sun turns his face away from the earth for a little while. That accounts for the eclipse. **These Yuchi may be known by the color of their skin, which is nearly black. The blackskinned Yuchi are the Sun's sons. There are a few living now.**[185]

In other words, the first man was a Black man, and the Black Yuchi, his direct descendants, were recognized as the "Original People." These Black people – like the "Little Black People" of Taiwan[186] or North Africa – were of great importance. If they disappeared, God would no longer be tied to the planet and the world would end.

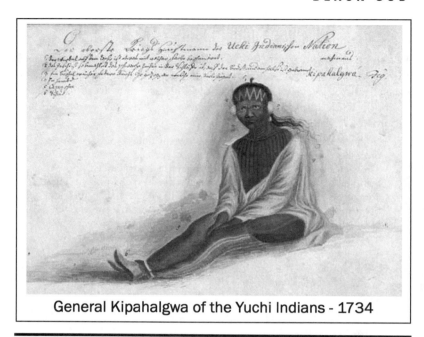

General Kipahalgwa of the Yuchi Indians - 1734

THE BLACK GODS OF THE AMERICAN SOUTHWEST

The American Southwest seems like an unlikely place to find gods who resemble Black men. Yet, somehow, we find them.

KOKOPELLI, THE GREAT HUNTER

Kokopelli is a well-known fertility god and hunter among the Hopi and Zuni people of the America southwest. As the spirit of fertility, he is seen as responsible for introducing corn (agriculture) to various peoples across the Americas. Kokopelli was first found in Anasazi rock carvings, but he also appears in Mississippian artifacts. Throughout South America, he is known as Ekoko. He is believed to descend from the Mayan Ekchuah. Kokopelli is identified with the southwestern Tewa people's god *Nepokwa'i*, a great hunter who is described as "a big black man."[187]

Xaman Ek and other Merchant Gods

Where did these Black gods come from? And how did a group of people who don't look African end up with gods who do? As always, they were once real people.

Leo Wiener provides a detailed account of the Black gods of Mexico in the third volume of his *Africa and the Discovery of America*, adding Mayan gods L and M, and high god Xaman Ek to the list.[188] Wiener traces these gods back to Black merchants trading prized goods like cacao, feathers, and animal skins, which they imported from afar.

Xaman Ek

In his *Yucatan Before and After the Conquest*, Diego de Landa says "Ekchuah is the recognized god of the merchants, the *beyom*, or 'traveling man.' At first, Ekchuah was a god of warriors, but became a beneficial god for merchants. The same story is told about the Black God M in Mexico.

Bishamon and Daikoku, two of the Black gods of Japan, share nearly the same story as that of Ekchuah. There are also stories of Black warrior/merchant gods in Europe and India, suggesting that ancient African traders traveled far and wide, establishing reputations of mythical proportions. These traditions appear to tell the story of the Africans who arrived in the Americas, first establishing themselves as formidable warriors, then as master traders, and perhaps finally as cultural leaders. This is almost certainly how the Black God Chaikwana came to be worshipped.

Chaikwana, the Traveler

The Native Americans of the American Southwest have more than one Black god. Chakwaina is a *kachina* (or divinity) of the Hopi, Zuni, and Keresan people (but not known by the Tewa, who have a Black god named *Nepokwa'i*). His dolls are spread throughout Pueblo culture, where he is usually painted black with yellow eyes.[189] Some anthropologists believed that Chakwaina was a ceremonial representation of Estevanico. But others argue that Chakwaina was known before this time.[190]

Drawing of Estevanico

Estevanico was the African Moor who led the ill-fated Narvaez expedition into North America. He led the four survivors as far west as modern Arizona, where they met the Hopi and Estevanico disappeared. Some say he was killed by the Zuni Indians for claiming. But another possibility is that he and his Indian friends *faked his death* so that he could go free and live among them.

Figure of Chaikwana

In fact, Estevanico may have been seen as a god or shaman. According to one source, "Estevan, who was black and wore feathers and rattles, may have looked like a wizard to the Zuni,"[191] while others note that he was identified with the southwestern god Chakwaina.[192]

LITTLE BLACK GODS ACROSS AMERICA

Some indigenous communities in the Americas have oral traditions regarding the presence of "little Black people" on the outskirts of their communities. The evidence suggests they knew these diminutive

Black people to be exceptional healers and medicine men.

For example, the Aztec god *Ixtlilton*, known as "the little negro," or "the black-faced," was the god of medicine and healing, and cured children of various diseases. He was also the god of feasting, dancing, and games. When Native American communities met with enslaved Africans between the 1600s and 1800s, they often became fast allies. These Africans were often highly revered, and it was said that they had "Great Medicine" in their bodies.

Ixtlilton

According to some accounts, this "Great Medicine" referred to the Africans' immunity to diseases like smallpox and malaria, to which most pure-blooded native people were highly vulnerable. By other accounts, however, "Great Medicine" meant "God," suggesting the Africans were – to use Five Percenter terminology – "godbody."

This may be how Black visitors came to be so highly respected in communities where they were otherwise considered "strangers." Outside of trade relationships (which were more common along the eastern coasts of Mexico), shamanism and the healing arts formed a vital bridge between Black and Native communities. In the second volume of his 1921 work, *Africa and the Discovery of America*, Leo Wiener writes:

> In the first volume I show that Negroes had a far greater influence upon American civilization than has heretofore been suspected. In the second volume I shall chiefly study the African fetishism, which even with the elaborate books on the subject, is woefully misunderstood, and I shall show by documentary evidence to what extraordinary extent the Indian medicine-man owes his evolution to the African medicine-man.

The Navajo story of Hastsezini is a testament to the respect given to such Black healers.

THE BLACK GOD OF THE NAVAHO

Among the Navaho, there is a deity known as Black God. He is not widely-celebrated, but he is very important because his knowledge of medicine saved the rest of the Navaho gods from certain death.

Black God is the Navajo god of fire. Perhaps because of this, he is also considered the creator of the stars. He is often depicted as black "like space" and wearing a crescent moon on his forehead, with the stars of Pleiades dotted on his temple. But Black God was most likely a medicine man before he came to be known as the god of fire. And he was not portrayed as Black because he symbolized space, but because he was most likely one of the Black men who brought a wealth of traditional knowledge over from West Africa.

Hastsezini

There are few records about him, but the following account is reclusive character who knows how to cure illnesses even the Indian gods cannot. But he won't take money. What does he want?

I'll let you read the story and see for yourself. You'll see why Black God was such an important, yet secretive, character, and how his medicinal knowledge – which is still used today – was the stuff of legend. The tale also explains why some indigenous people in the Americas paint themselves black in certain rituals – perhaps in commemoration of men like Hastsezini.

THE BLACK GOD AND THE SACRED CIGARETTE

At the Twelfth Annual Meeting of the American Folk-Lore Society in 1901, ethnographer Washington Matthews retold a "rite-myth" of the Navaho Indians of New Mexico and Arizona. Rite-myths, he explained, tell the story of how different rites and ceremonies came to be practiced by groups like the Navaho.

"I shall relate to you now," he continued, "in the words of a shaman, a brief myth of how a couple of the greatest divinities of the Navaho pantheon were taken ill and how they were successfully treated by a minor divinity." Matthews begins:

> It is long since the Navahoes went to war; but in former days when we fought our enemies we often suffered from war diseases. Our young men know nothing of this. One who killed an enemy by striking him in the chest would get disease in the chest; one who killed his enemy by striking on the head would get disease of the head, and one who killed by wounding in the abdomen would get disease of that part.

WHAT DOES THE BLACK GOD WANT?

This "war disease" made the gods so weak they could barely function. Nothing would cure it. Now, we don't know if the "war disease" referred to cancer or some other condition that can affect different parts of the body. What we know is that there is still a rite that aims to treat or prevent such ailments, and this rite was introduced by a mysterious Black character. The story continues:

> At length some one said: "There is one dwelling at Tse'sindiai (Black Standing Rock) named Dontso (an insect) who knows of one who can cure war disease." So the people lay in wait for Dontso and caught him. "Who is it that can cure the war disease?" they asked. "I dare not tell," said Dontso; "it is one whom I fear, who does not like to have his power known." But the people persisted and persuaded and threatened till at last Dontso said: "It is Hastsezini (Black God), the owner of all fire. But never let him know it was I who revealed the secret, for I fear his vengeance."

This passage should give you some clue as to the level of secrecy associated with Black Gods in some parts of the world.

When the people learned of Hastsezini, they "got a sacred buckskin, filled it with jewelled baskets, precious stones, shells, feathers, and all the treasures the gods most prize, and sent the bundle by a messenger to Hastsesini." But when the messenger arrived at the god's home and presented his bundle, the fire-god only said, "Begone! Go home, and take your bundle with you."

The messenger returned to his people and told them what happened. They tried again, several times, each time adding more wealth to their offering. Each time, the messenger was rejected. The Black God wanted none of the things the other gods prized. He didn't even rise from his seat on the floor before sending the messenger away.

THE SACRED CIGARETTE

Finally, Dontso asked the people what they had offered him.

> "He is not like other gods," said Dontso; "he is surly and exclusive. Few of the holy ones ever visit him, and he rarely visits any one. He cares nothing for your sacred buckskins, your baskets of turquoise and white shell, your abalone and rock crystal. All he wants is a smoke, but his cigarette must be made in a very particular way." And then he told them how to make the cigarette sacred to Hastsezini. But he made the people all pledge secrecy. He lived with the fire-god, and thus he came to know how the cigarette should be made and how it should be given to the god.

Matthews doesn't explain what goes into the "cigarette" or how it is made, and adds that the Navajos meant to keep it a secret as well.

When the messenger delivered this "sacred cigarette" to the Black God, he took it, examined it, and said angrily, "Who taught you to make this cigarette? No one knows how to make it but Hastiniasi (Little Old Man) and Dontso. One of these must have taught you." The messenger doesn't reveal the secret of who taught him. Eventually, the Black God gives him a chance:

> Hastsezini examined the cigarette again, inhaled its odor four times, and said: "Laa! It is well! This is my cigarette. Stay you and show me the way I must travel. Let the other messengers go home in advance. I shall get there on the morning of the third day."

If you ask me, it looks like all the brother wanted was a properly rolled joint. But that's just my theory.

Whatever it was that he smoked, the Black God was satisfied. He agreed to come to the people, but they begged him to come sooner. So he told them about the kind of feast he wanted, and they began putting it together. The story continues:

> Next morning the Black God left his home, went about half way to Nayenezgani's house, and camped for the night. Many people came to his camp and held a dance there. There were birds among them, for in those days birds were people. And because of this occurrence now, in our day, when Hastsezini camps at night on his way to the medicine-lodge, the people go to his camp and hold a dance.
>
> On the morning after this dance, all left for the house of sickness and got there at sunset. Before they arrived they began to shout and to whoop. The Navahoes in these days shout and whoop, and they call this shouting altsitse. A party from Nayenezgani's house, when they heard the shouting, went out to meet the returning party, and they had a mock battle, in which Hastsezini's party seemed victorious. Such a mock battle we hold today in the rites.

Thus, many of the important Navaho traditions were born. The

Black God then taught them to make a medicinal charcoal from plants and minerals, which they would rub on their bodies until their skin "looked as black as that of Hastsezini himself."

This, along with a cold infusion and several other treatments, left the Navaho gods "happily restored" and fully healed. Thus, this process became part of the Navaho healing tradition. The shaman who told the story concluded, "As was done to the gods then, so would we do to-day, if one among us got the war-disease."[193]

THE ORIGIN OF FIRE

Among the Jicarilla Apache, the origin of fire, home-building, and hunting are all traced back to an important figure known as Haschĭn Dĭlhĭli, or "Black Man." This is the beginning of that myth, as told by Edward Curtis in *The North American Indian*:

> Black Man, Haschĭn Dĭlhĭli, was created by Nayĕnayĕzganĭ to be his helper in the task of making the earth a good dwelling-place for the people. Haschĭn made the animals, mountains, trees, and rivers, gave the people weapons and implements, and showed how they were to be used. When all were supplied with houses to live in and weapons with which to protect themselves and to kill game, he called Coyote, Tsilitĕn, the Mimic.[194]

Coyote then has Little Tree help him steal fire from an underground community of fireflies. He then runs from home to home, until every human family is supplied with fire.

THE BLACK CREATOR OF THE APACHE

The Jicarilla Apache also recognize a group of mythical figures known as the Hactcin, who are described as "the only beings of the beginnings when nothing existed, yet they possessed all necessary for the creation of the universes and all pertaining to it."[195]

The most powerful of these gods was known as Black Hactcin (essentially "Black God"). In *Creation Myths of the World*, David Adams Leeming writes:

> The Hactcin existed before creation, when there was only dark, wet chaos – the world womb, as it were. Being lonely, the Hactcin created the essential elements of the universe and also created Earth Mother and Sky Father. As for the people, at this time they lived

only as a potential form in the damp dark underworld, where a figure called Black Hactcin rules. Black Hactcin was the true creator.[196]

According to Dr. Harold Fuchs, Black Hactcin created the original animal and bird from which all others derived, as well as man and woman.[197] In Richard Willows' summary of the Jicarilla creation story, man is made to take the place of the departing Black Creator:

> In the beginning, there was nothing, but darkness, water, and moving wind. Nothing lived except for the eternal spirits. These Spirits had great power. **The strongest of these spirits was Black Hactcin**. Together he and all the spirits made the Earth, yet he alone made all the birds and animals that lived upon it. One day however, Black Hactcin announced that he couldn't stay forever, so all the animals begged him to make **someone similar to Hactcin to take his place** and keep them company. So Hactcin ordered them to go gather materials from around the world to make man. When they were gathering all the materials, Black Hactcin turned them into man.[198]

The Black God then blew "wind" into this man to animate him. This man would resemble and represent the Black God who made him.

THE POPOL VUH

The *Popol Vuh* has been described as "one of the rarest relics of aboriginal thought."[199] It has been subtitled *The Sacred Book of the Ancient Quiche Maya*,[200] but a literal translation of the title would be *The Book of the People*. The *Popol Vuh* contains the popular traditions and mythology of the Mayans who lived in present day Guatemala after the fall of the Maya Old Empire.

The Quiche say the *Popol Vuh* is indeed an old book which ancient kings and lords would draw upon for inspiration as well as prophecy and divination. It was first transcribed into Latin script in the Quiche language sometime between 1554 and 1558. Before this, it was preserved by a long history of oral tradition. The "original tradition" is said to have existed "long ago; but its sight is [now] hidden from the searcher and the thinker."[201]

Numerous versions of the book exist now, each offering slight differences in wording and interpretation. The version I purchased in Mexico describes the first man being made from black clay. The author says this first man was imperfect, "however, the new creature had the gift of speech and sounded more harmonious than any music that had ever been heard before under the heavens."[202]

Though the gods would continue to make three more races of man before finally arriving at one with which they were satisfied (the second and third were violently destroyed), the first, the Black race, was allowed to live and given time to multiply and "improve their kind." This is interesting, as I haven't found any mention of an original Black race in the translations I've come across in the U.S.

Scholars have noted a line of cultural transmission from the Mayan people to the Indians of the American southwest. The *Popol Vuh*'s original Black race may have some relation to the Southwest Indian story of the Emergence, a story Runoko Rashidi says "is as important in the region as the Book of Genesis is to Christians." In this creation story, the First World is called the Black World.[203]

THE HOPI PROPHECY

Lee Brown, a Salish Indian from British Columbia, Canada, had lived and studied among the Hopi for several years. In 1986, he gave a talk at the Continental Indigenous Council that should not be ignored.

Brown begins with a commentary on the races of the Earth, expressing a strong solidarity with Black people:

> A medicine man from South Dakota put a beaded medicine wheel in the middle of the gathering. It had the four colors from the four directions. He asked the people, "Where is this from?" They said, "Probably Montana, or South Dakota, maybe Saskatchewan." He said, "This is from Kenya." It was beaded just like ours, with the same color… Always we were trying to live together. But instead of living together, you all know there was separation, there was segregation. They separated the races: they separated the Indians, and they separated the blacks.

What he says afterwards is especially significant:

> In 1776 when the United States Government printed the dollar, in one claw [of the eagle], if you've ever noticed, there is an olive branch in this claw. They said that represented peace. The Indian elders shared with me in South Dakota that to them that represents the enslavement of black people. In the prophecies of the Six Nations people they say there will be two great uprisings by black people to free themselves. We've seen one about 1964…There was one more uprising coming for the black race of people and then they will be released and this is also going to have an effect on Native people, a good effect. There's a whole new set of prophecies from the Iroquois people about that and I won't have time to go into that this morning.

I can only *imagine* how much more there is to this prophecy. Actually, that's not entirely true. I know exactly what comes next.

BLACK GODS OF THE U.S.

A REVOLUTIONARY THEOLOGY

"Man Know Thyself! When you know yourself then you will know God or Elohim." – Father George Hurley, 1923

The ideas discussed in this book are not new. They've been suppressed, ignored, or dismissed, but they are worthy of our serious consideration. If nothing else can be said about them, these ideas have struck fear into the hearts of many. Why? Perhaps because of the power they hold and the truths they may reveal.

THE MODERN BLACK GOD

As many of us know, the idea of a "Black God" is especially prominent in the theology of the Nation of Islam and the Five Percenters (or Nation of Gods and Earths). What is less known, however, is the long history of this teaching here in the U.S.

THE "GREAT BLACK GOD" WHO SORTS OUT THE WICKED

In 1920, George Kibbe Turner published *Hagar's Hoard*, where Turner reported on aspects of Black theology that few Americans were aware of:

> You can say what you want to, about the niggers, but they're a mighty religious race. The only thing is that what they believe – the ordinary run of them – is so mighty strange and different from other folks. They won't ever tell about it much, if they can help it – only fool you. But sometimes, when you get one right, you can get him to tell you some things they really do believe, way down under.
>
> They believe, every one of them, they're God's people, just like the old Jews. And they believe, in a kind of way, that the Old Bible is talking about them when it talks about the Jews. And King Solomon was a black man. They'll show you that right there in the Bible. And some of them, I know for certain, say Christ was black; and I believe – yes, I know – there's plenty of them think that God is black – a big black God, watching specially after His black people,

and punishing their enemies and oppressors.

> And every now and then, there's one of them, like I say, gets up and prophesies – a woman generally. And a big cloud's coming up, and the winds will blow and the trumpets. And the black angels will rise out of the ground, and the sinful city will be destroyed; or the old sinful world will come to an end – and the great black God will sort out the wicked and righteous forever.[204]

Even today, these ideas are intimidating for many. Who would imagine that Black people believed such things in the 1920s, almost a full century ago? Where did these ideas come from?

BLACK GODS OF THE METROPOLIS

In *Black Gods of the Metropolis: Negro Cults of the Urban North*, originally published in 1944, Arthur Huff Fauset outlines the history of Black men being revered as gods in the United States. Fauset, an important Black anthropologist and Civil Rights activist, covers the development of widespread movements surrounding Messianic Black figures like:

Noble Drew Ali, who founded the Moorish Science Temple of America in Newark in 1913,

Prophet Cherry, who founded the Church of God, a congregation of Black Jews, in Philadelphia in 1915 (and who may have been teaching even earlier in Tennessee)

Father Divine, who founded the Peace Mission in New York City around 1919, which attracted hordes of white followers,

Father George W. Hurley, who founded Universal Hagar's Spiritual Church, in Detroit in 1923, which embraced esoteric sciences

Would it be fair to call these congregations "cults," as if their "Messianic" leaders were simply preachers who wanted to be worshipped as gods? Not necessarily. As Benjamin Sevitch reports in a study titled "When Black Gods Preached on Earth":

> These men are God to their people, the black God who has come to deliver black people from white rule. In this, the cult-type does not fall between the black church or sect types, but transcends them.[205]

Several of these men taught their followers that they, too, could find their God in the mirror. Father Divine was one of the few who taught that only he was God, but his mentor Father Jehovia, had preached "I am God" but that the "indwelling of God's spirit" was also in "everyman." Hurley, who called himself "The Black God of the Aquarian Age," also told his followers, "Man Know Thyself! When you know yourself then you will know God or Elohim." This sort of tradition has been carried on into the present day.

Next question: Would it be fair to say that these teachings began in the urban centers of the North? No. Many of these men had migrated to the North in the Great Migration. Some of them were teaching their theology before they'd left the South.

How far back, then, can these teachings be traced? Most of these men were first taught or mentored by individuals about whom we have very little information. Some scholars have suggested that the New Thought movement of the early 1900s (popularized by authors like James Allen and William Walker Atkinson) played a role in spreading these ideas to Black communities. It may be true that Father Divine and some others drew on New Thought philosophy from time to time, but this tradition was much older than New Thought.

BLACK THEOLOGY IN THE 1700S

If you've read the rest of the *Science of Self* series, you know that these teachings aren't new. They've been around for thousands of years. But when do we first find such teaching in the United States? We have to dig into the historical records to find the earliest accounts. In the following excpet from *The Science of Self, Volume One*, we tell much of the story that hasn't really been told:

> By the late 1700s, educated brothers like Prince Hall (the founder of the Prince Hall Masons) and Richard Allen (founder of the African Methodist Episcopal Church) were teaching Black people to study their past and respect their heritage. They hinted that Blacks occupied a special place in the universe, but left much unsaid.

Judging from the traditions these two inspired, Hall and Allen must have known something especially profound. But why did they leave so much unsaid? Perhaps because it was the 1700s! You couldn't simply go around saying "God is a Black man" or "The Black man is God" …without being murdered barbarically.

DAVID WALKER'S APPEAL

Still, others found the zeal to say what needed to be said:

> In 1829, David Walker published his infamous *Appeal*, which spoke of the "God of the Blacks" in opposition with "heathen" whites "acting like devils," and the idea that "your full glory and happiness, as well as all other coloured people under Heaven, shall never be fully consummated, but with the *entire emancipation of your enslaved brethren all over the world.*"

It is no coincidence that Walker relied on both the Prince Hall

Masons (who published his book) and the AME Church (who provided him other resources) to spread his message, which eventually made its way into the Deep South, where it inspired several slave revolts.

Even Nat Turner may have been inspired by receiving Walker's word. Many of these revolts came directly out of AME churches. Once the Appeal was traced back to its author, Walker's life was in constant danger. He was eventually killed by poisoning. Fortunately, we know about his life because his published work has survived.

A BLACK MASTER OF THE ESOTERIC

In other cases, we don't know much about who was teaching what. For example, in the late 1800s, there was an important occultist named Paschal Beverly Randolph. He founded the first Rosicrucian order in the United States, and was widely noted for his esoteric knowledge. H.P. Blavatsky "borrowed" quite a bit from him to found her school of Theosophy. She also hated him. Why? Randolph was a Black man. And, as discretely as he could (considering this was the 1800s), he was teaching a revolutionary theology.

Despite his discretion, he said quite more than any Black man could at the time – partly because very few people knew that he was Black, as he kept this fact a secret. In his 1868 work, *After Death: The Disembodiment of Man*, Randolph wrote that the first man must have been a Black man, and that the original man "like God, had no conceivable beginning." The "grand secret of the ages," Randolph said, was that God had breathed himself into man. The soul of man, he taught, was "indivisible" from the Eternal creator. In other words, man and God were one.*

THE AME AND BISHOP TURNER

Meanwhile, the AME Church remained committed to a responsible Black theology more appropriate for the mainstream Christian community. They emphasized the divine connection between God and the Black man, but didn't publicly reveal much more than that. By the 1890s, however, things were heating up. Prominent AME Bishop Henry McNeal Turner went ahead and put it all the way out there, proclaiming that God himself "was a Negro."

In the following years, the emergence of Ethiopist traditions in the

---

* We'll revisit Randolph and his teachings in a future book, dedicated to the world's secret societies and what they 'really' teach.

Black church turned the attention of Black Christians back toward their African roots, and eventually towards Black conceptions of Christ. This development gave way to Pan-African movements like that of Marcus Garvey in the early 1900s.

THE BLACK GOD OF MARCUS GARVEY

In *Black Moses*, a history of Marcus Garvey and the UNIA, E. David Cronon writes:

> Indeed, many religious cults and sects among American Negroes had projected the idea of a black God long before Garvey had arrived in the United States. Even some whites had suggested that Black ministers should think in black terms and one fastidious southerner had even asserted that the Negro's Bible "ought to teach him that he will become a black angel and will go home at death to a black God."

In other words, Garvey wasn't the first to teach Americans of a Black God, but he may have been the most successful. At the height of his career, Marcus Mosiah Garvey taught over two million Black men and women that God was Black and that Black was beautiful.

Garvey also pulled in other theologians to push this teaching. William Henry Ferris, an AME pastor with an Ivy League background, soon became the UNIA's Chairman, and contributed heavily to Garvey's speechwriting. In 1913, he published a phenomenal two-volume series titled *The African Abroad*, where Ferris explored a wealth of evidence that Blacks built most of the world's ancient civilizations, the lives of great Black leaders, and the idea of man as God, and God as man.

Garvey also recruited Reverend George Alexander McQuire, a prominent Episcopalian clergyman who left his post to become Chaplain General of the UNIA. Bishop McGuire, now head of the African Orthodox Church, told his congregation to "forget the white gods." On another occasion he is quoted preaching, "Erase the white gods from your heart. We must go back to the native church, to our own true God."

Many – both Black and white alike – opposed Garvey's theology. Yet this idea of God was one that could not be repressed. Instead, it spread. In 1923, W.E.B. Du Bois published *Darkwater*, where he prayed for the rise of a Black Messiah, and for God to bring the end of white rule. Who would have thought?

REVOLUTIONARY SOUTHERN THEOLOGY

This revolutionary Black theology – the same one George Kibbe

Turner talks about above – wasn't limited to the North. The same year *Hagar's Hoard* was published, Stephen Graham published *Children of the Slaves*, where he reported that wealthy Blacks in Alabama were manufacturing Black dolls to promote racial pride. This fact is important, as this beginning of this book. Why were these people proud to be Black? Why did they want their children to identify with their blackness? Graham, like other whites, was perplexed by this phenomenon. After learning of the "race pride" that went into making these dolls, Graham met with a Black preacher in Birmingham. In Graham's account, his conversation with Reverend Williams went as follows:

"Now, isn't it absurd for us to have white angels?" the Reverend asked Graham.

"You surely would not like them black?" Graham replied.

Reverend Williams explained, "We give Sunday-school cards to our children with white angels on them. It's *wrong.*"

"Black angels would be ugly," Graham said.

"No more ugly than white," the Reverend shot back

At this point, you can imagine what Graham was thinking. He most likely didn't expect to have such a conversation, especially not in southern Birmingham. He continues:

> I thought the whiteness of the angels was as the whiteness of white light which contained all colour. That, however, was lost on the Reverend, who happened to be a realist.
>
> "Christ himself was not white. He would have had to travel in a Jim Crow car," said he. "But put it to yourself: isn't it absurd for us to be taught that the good are all white, and that sin itself is black?"
>
> "It does seem to leave you in the shade," said I.
>
> "Expressions such as 'black as sin' ought to be deleted from the language. One might as well say 'white as sin.'"
>
> I ransacked my brain rapidly. "We say 'pale as envy,'" said I.
>
> "Black spite,'" he retorted. "Why should it be black?"
>
> I could not say. [206]

Graham was at a loss for words. Reverend Williams, seeing that he was winning his argument, pushed forward even further:

> "Then Adam and Eve in the Garden," he went on, "are always shown as beautifully white creatures, whereas, considering the climate, they may well have been as dark-skinned as any Negro couple in Alabama. Babylon itself was built by Negroes." [207]

Graham wonders if the good Reverend is saying that the Black man was the original man. He asks, "Would you have Adam and Eve painted black?" Quite seriously, the Reverend responds, "Why, yes, I would."

Clearly, when it came to revolutionary Black theology, the South was definitely in the house.

"GETTING BUSY ON A BLACK GOD"

I can only imagine the look on Graham's face when the good Reverend told him these things. This would not, however, be the last of his surprises:

> Later, in New York one night at Liberty Hall, before I was driven out as a white interloper, I heard an orator say to an admiring host of Negroes: "Why, I ask you, is God always shown as white? It is because He is the white man's God. It is the God of our masters. (Yes, brother, that's it.) It's the God of those who persecute and despise the coloured people. Brothers, we've got to knock that white God down and put up a black God – we've got to re-write the Old Testament and the New from a black man's point of view. Our theologians must get busy on a black God."[208]

From the 1920s forward, this is exactly what theologians get busy on. In *The Science of Self*, we continue:

> The UNIA's widespread influence helped facilitate the rise of Noble Drew Ali's Moorish Science Temple in the 1920s. The Moorish Science Temple, in turn, with its emphasis on the "science" of the Asiatic Blackman and his "hidden" history, opened the doors of Black American consciousness to Islam. When Wallace Fard Muhammad introduced the theology of what was then known as the Allah Temple of Islam to Detroit in 1934, it was like nothing the people had heard before…yet still not entirely unfamiliar.[209]

"BLACKS DON'T WANT A WHITE GOD"

The American Missionary Association was a nondenominational Christian educational society founded by a network of Black and white abolitionists in 1846. They fought for Black freedom, before and after the abolition of slavery. In a 1928 edition of their publication *The American Missionary*, there's a passage titled, "Blacks Don't Want a White God." It reads, in part:

> The colored races of the world are working out a new religion; one that will not come short of the ideals and noble ethical principles of Jesus. When that religion shall have been completely worked out, they will have to find a new name for it other than Christianity: I mean "white-man Christianity." If you doubt this, study more closely the youth movements in China, India, Japan and Africa.[210]

This "new" theology was much like the "old" theology we can now uncover in the ancient remains of the Egypt, India, or Mesoamerica.

It's almost as if things were coming full circle. In ancient times, learned initiates would come to find that the God worshipped by the common people was not to be found on a mountain or in the heavens above, but in the mirror. This was the secret kept in all the ancient temples and mystery schools.

In the most distant past, however, the knowledge of God was not a temple secret. It was understood by indigenous people in such a way that it rarely needed to be said. To return to the ways of our ancestors, the knowledge of God had to become widely known.

REAWAKENING TODAY'S BLACK GODS

In *The Science of Self*, we explain how this happened, detailing the "revolutionary curriculum" introduced by Master Fard Muhammad, who – with the Honorable Elijah Muhammad – founded the Nation of Islam in the 1930s.

In 1964, a member of the NOI, then named Clarence 13X, left the temple to share this revolutionary curriculum with the masses, specifically targeting Harlem's street youth:

> These street youth became known as the Five Percenters, who – after Allah's assassination – embraced a "free culture" approach with no formal leadership, a model whose closest precursors were the indigenous cultures of Native American and African societies.
>
> The Five Percenters took the NOI's curriculum and minimized the religious emphasis of its teachings, emphasizing the analysis and investigation of everything found within the Supreme Wisdom lessons (which they renamed "120 Degrees") and added the study of Supreme Mathematics (a symbolic system of numerical laws) and Supreme Alphabet (a related system of principles) as decoding tools.
>
> Through often intense exchanges that would have put Socrates and his peers to shame, growing circles of teenage Five Percenters developed a new framework through which they could understand themselves and their relationships with the universe in which they lived, and pass these teachings on to ever-increasing numbers of people in the streets.[211]

THE SEVENTH SEAL REVEALED

Five Percenters do not typically publish literature. Since their inception, theirs has been primarily an oral tradition, like other indigenous cultures across the world. Sometimes, reputable Five Percenters have published their writings, but these writings weren't made widely available to outsiders. You simply had to "come around" the community, just as you'd expect with an indigenous tradition preserving some serious knowledge.

A few years after I first immersed myself in this culture on the streets of Jersey City, I came across a photocopied essay, titled "The Mystery of the Seventh Seal." In it, Shabazz Adew Allah explains how this seal of secrecy was broken, revealing "once and for all the final mystery of God: That the Blackman, Supreme and all wise is the Almighty true and living God." He writes:

> According to those in the know, the teaching that God (Allah) is the Black Man is as old as the universe itself. From the Pope in Rome to the Shariff of Mecca, to the Grand Lama in Tibet, knowledge relating to the identity and origin of these Black Gods is commonly known, but is kept mutually suppressed. That the true and living God and the one referred to in the secret chambers of Freemasonry as the "Great Architect of the Universe" is none other than the Blackman is a recognized fact long acknowledged by the heads of the world's religious orders.

> Yet for thousands of years, these religious leaders i.e. Popes, Imams, and Rabbis alike have conspired to keep this knowledge hidden from the world at large. Among Christians and Muslims, Freemasons and Jewish Cabalists, and within the Temples of Tibetan Monks and the Mystery Lodges of Ancient Egypt, this was the one unspeakable truth which formed the core of their esoteric teachings.

Adew continues, explaining that this knowledge of God was either forgotten or repressed, but has – since 1964 – been exposed to the masses in a way that was unheard of for thousands of years.

"Behold, I will send my messenger, and he shall prepare the way before me: and the Lord, whom ye seek, shall suddenly come to his temple, even the messenger of the covenant, whom ye delight in: behold, he shall come, saith the LORD of hosts." – Malachi 3:1

He credits Allah and the Five Percenters (also known as the Nation of Gods and Earths) with ushering in this "open access" era of revelation.[212] All one had to do is "come around." He concludes:

> In these, the last days of the European presence as the ruling power upon our planet, the knowledge of self and the science of life is being freely and openly disseminated to the masses by the Five Percent Nation of the Gods and Earths, teaching that the Blackman is the real Father of civilization and true God of the universe. These Gods (Men) and Earths (Woman) are building to awaken the people from their mental death.

In ancient times, this knowledge was preserved by mystics, priests, shamans, kings, and scribes. Today, this ancient knowledge is found preserved as it was when it began, in oral tradition. To find it, one has to "come around."

"But in the days of the voice of the seventh angel, when he shall begin to sound, the mystery of God should be finished, as he hath declared to his servants the prophets." – Revelation 10:7

REVIEW

What do most of the Black gods in this book have in common? In most cases, their stories appear to be a mix of history and myth. To be clear, by "myth" we simply mean the kind of associations that can make a mortal man seem immortal. The stuff that makes one seem worthy of worship, fear, or adoration, long after their physical death.

Across the board, these Black gods are usually based on a combination of two elements:

1.) a natural, social, or scientific principle (like the light of the sun, political leadership, or the knowledge of agriculture), and

2.) a historical personality who became identified with that principle.

This is true for many gods, even if we haven't fully figured out who the historical figure was. After all, some of these myths are thousands of years old, while others are even older. You can imagine that some stories have been crossed, merged, mixed up, and some have almost certainly lost a few things in translation over the centuries. After all, even our written scriptures have seen their fair share of "editing," so we can only guess how much the oral traditions have changed.

Yet there's still great consistency in most of these stories. The Black man identified in the Mayan Codices as "God L" is portrayed as a trader in almost every codex where he's found. And he's not the only Black god associated with trade. Why? Because Black men went around the world in ancient times, doing trade. And they were amazing men. Amazing enough, apparently, to be worthy of oral traditions and cultural reverence, which, over generations, can become myth and worship.

However, as Shabazz Adew Allah writes in "The Mystery of the Seventh Seal":

> As generation succeeded generation, the memory of these ancient Gods, who walked, taught, and loved in the land, became dimmer and dimmer. There soon came a time when the true accounts of these Black Gods were repeatedly forgotten, and only vague recollections of their past ventures remained, mainly as myths, legends, and fairy tales. Yet we know from the writing in the ancient scrolls, monuments, and temples that these Gods actually walked the Earth as they do nowadays. Praised, worshipped and glorified as the bestowers of civilization, these Black Gods are still honored and secretly adored in many lands.

These Black gods were not all alike, nor were they entirely different.

In this section, we'll review the various "character types" of Black gods we've found throughout the world, and why these types exist.

LEADERS

Let's begin with the obvious. We know that kings and great leaders were often treated like gods on Earth. Often, there was a cultural tradition that explained this divine connection between an "earthly" ruler and a "heavenly" ruler. In other cases, a history of great works could earn them a sort of "cult following" after their death.

Question: In this book, how many Gods were based on the worship of great leaders and rulers?

ANCESTORS

Often, whoever is identified as a community's "progenitor" (the one who fathered everyone) attains some sort of divine status in their community, if not being regarded as an incarnation of God on Earth. In fact, any ancestor who contributed to the greatness of that community can earn some sort of cult following. Also, communities of people (like the DBP) who were understood to be the "first people" were often considered sacred or divine. Sometimes, settlers who were not familiar with the history of their region's DBP became fearful of their power because of the mythology associated with them.

Question: How many of the Black gods discussed in this book were based on ancestors, progenitors, and the "original people"?

TRAVELLING TEACHERS

When I say that many of the world's Black gods were based on Black men who had travelled from afar, it wasn't simply that they had travelled from distant lands. The reverence they earned was based on what they did when they got to these new lands. Often, they introduced new traditions, such as the Anu Cultural Complex, which essentially "saved" communities from running out of food and other resources when the climate shifted.

According to Greek historian Diodorus Sicilus, the great "ancestor god" Osiris left Nubia and continued his migration up the Nile Valley to found civilizations in Asia:

> From Ethiopia he (Osiris) passed through Arabia, bordering upon the Red Sea as far as to India, and the remotest inhabited coasts; he

built likewise many cities in India, one of which he called Nysa, willing to have a remembrance of that (Nysa) in Egypt where he was brought up. At this Nysa in India he planted ivy, which continues to grow here, but nowhere else in India or near it. He left likewise many other marks of his being in those parts, by which the latter inhabitants are induced to believe, and do affirm, that this god was born in India. He likewise addicted himself much to the hunting of elephants, and took care to have statues of himself in every place, as lasting monuments of his expedition.

In other words, Ausar (Osiris) – who symbolizes the Anu people – left Nubia to establish Anu civilizations in Egypt, Arabia, and then India.

Question: Which of the Black gods in this book were "culture heroes," "teachers of the arts," and "founders of civilization"? Why did they come to teach?

TRADERS AND MERCHANTS

In places where we find Black gods being worshipped as a "god of the merchants" or a "god of prosperity," we're seeing this connection because of a Black man who most likely traveled into that community, stood out because of his distinct features or personality, and still managed to introduce highly coveted goods or foods (and often the techniques on how to produce these things locally).

Question: How many of this book's gods fit this description? What did they sell or trade, and why where these items so important?

WARRIORS

Wherever there's been a history of military conflict and conquest, you'll find Black gods revered as the most excellent warriors. In some cases, they are the root of the entire warrior tradition. Particularly in those places where there was a racial conflict between Black and white communities, you'll find Black gods first being rendered as warriors, but later being described in such fearful terms that they become demonized as "wicked" characters.

Question: Which of this book's gods fit this description? What were they guarding, defending, or fighting for?

HEALERS

While some Black "warrior gods" were associated with pestilence and sickness, many of the world's Black gods were credited for having great powers in healing and medicine. As we can find many examples of shamans, healers, "medicine men," and so-called "witch doctors" being revered as divine, even in indigenous communities today. In some cases, these people were known to have the power to take away disease, but also to inflict it on those who were wicked.

Question: Which of this book's gods fit the "healer" description? What do they have in common?

SAVIORS

What about those deities who seem to simply symbolize some aspect of the sun, moon, and stars? It's hard to associate their stories with an actual person, as we find the same myths all over the world. Why?

In some cases, there wasn't a historical person who became revered as a "Sun God" or "Savior" figure. Instead, these traditions might have been adopted from an older community who had an even older tradition. This is why there are so many myths across neighboring civilizations that share similarities, like the sixteen-plus "crucified saviors" described by Kersey Graves, or the many "Black Madonna" figures identified by Ean Begg.

Digging deeper, however, these myths may go back to a much older root. Over 200 years ago, Count C.F. Volney suggested that many of our shared myths could be traced back to our ancestors' understanding of celestial phenomena.

That is, they studied and tracked the stars to understand the seasons and other natural patterns (like the migrations of different animals), and they encoded their findings in the language of myth. Wherever we cannot be sure that an actual person traveled from one place to another – or that his worship was carried around – this theory can explain why there are great similarities in the traditions of different civilizations across the globe.

Addressing whether the Black Christ came to India or if the Black Krishna came to Europe, Godfrey Higgins chooses neither option. Instead, he says they are local versions of the same story, explaining:

> I must now request my reader to turn back to the first chapter, and to reconsider what I have said respecting the two Ethiopias and the existence of a *black* nation in a very remote period. When he has done this, the circumstance of the black God of India being called *Cristna,* and the God of Italy, *Christ,* being also black, must appear worthy of deep consideration. Is it possible, that this coincidence can have been the effect of accident?

Questions: Which of the gods described in this book share similarities with other deities in another part of the world? Why do you think this is so? Was it a historical connection, or simply a shared mythology? Is there a connection between any of these ancient gods and the conditions of the present?

Higgins believes that these myths were all somehow based on a much older root tradition. He encourages us to find this original tradition, which he calls a "lost science":

> In our endeavours to recover the lost science of former ages, it is necessary that we should avail ourselves of rays of light scattered in places the most remote, and that we should endeavour to re-collect them into a focus, so that, by this means, we may procure as strong a light as possible...

Questions: What is the "root tradition" that some esoteric authors call the "book of life"? What are the basic principles of this tradition?

In my opinion, the tradition of the Five Percent is as close as one can get to this root tradition. And today's "saviors" may be just as real as the savior gods of the ancient past. After all, the story of Christ may simply be the story of a real historical revolutionary, blended with the solar mythology we find everywhere else.

2,000 years from now, could one of us be revered in the same way? What "types" of gods does the world need today? Who will fulfill these roles? Who will they talk about 2,000 years from now?

What should you do now that you're done reading?
Here are some suggestions:

❏ Complete any activities mentioned in this book, especially the discussions. See any of the films mentioned, but with others.

❏ Tell somebody about this book and what you've learned. Invite them to come read it. Don't let them steal the book.

❏ As another option, let them steal the book. It might help them.

❏ Mentor some young people or teach a class using this book as a handbook or reference.

❏ Talk about this book online, but don't stay on the Net forever.

❏ Join an organization or group that discusses concepts like the ones in this book and get into those discussions.

❏ Leave this book away somewhere it will be picked up and read.

❏ Identify the people in your community who could use a copy of this book. If they're people would want to buy a book like this, let em read a few pages and see if they can afford to buy a copy.

❏ If they're people who don't normally buy books – but you know that givin em a copy could change their life – give em a copy and tell em to come see you when they're ready for another one. This is why you can order copies at wholesale rates at our site.

We hope this helps you keep the knowledge contagious.

ENDNOTES

SO YOU KNOW IT'S NOT ALL MADE UP

"You think the gods are dead. The gods never die." —
Gods by Shaw Desmond, 1921

I told you, I can't stand books with sketchy sources. What's worse is books that are supposed to be "nonfiction"...with NO sources. So I don't write anything unless I've got some documentation to back it up, and I do my best to make sure you know how to find my sources.

With that said, I'll admit I take shortcuts when it comes to citing my sources. It's definitely not ALA, Chicago, or Turabian style. Perhaps it's because I hate all the stuff you gotta dig up to cite a source properly. Or maybe I think nobody's gonna care either way. Typically, I'm just gonna give you the author, the title, and the year it came out. One thing's for sure, if you take the time to look up my sources, you'll see I'm not making stuff up. Can't say the same for some of these other guys...

1 Godfrey Higgins. (1833). Anacalypsis, Vol. 1. To be republished by Two Horizons Press in 2014.
2 Kenneth P. Clark and Mamie P. Clark. (1947). Racial Identification and Preference in Negro Children.
http://i2.cdn.turner.com/cnn/2010/images/05/13/doll.study.1947.pdf
3 Hazel Trice Edney. (Sep. 14 2006). "New Doll Test Produces Ugly Results." The Final Call. www.finalcall.com
4 T.W. MacMahon. (1862). Cause and Contrast: An Essay on the American Crisis. Gale Cengage Learning, p. 1, 36.
5 W. Crooke. (March 1900). "Legends of Krishna." Folklore: Transactions of the Folklore Society. Vol. 11, No. 1.
6 Elizabeth Hamilton. (1811). Translation of the letters of a Hindoo Rajah. P. vi.
7 Exotic India. (2013). "Why is Krishna Black?"
www.exoticindiaart.com/product/sculptures/why-is-krishna-black-RN03/
8 Lionel David Barnett. (1922). Hindu Gods And Heroes. Library of Alexandria.
9 Cited in Wesley Muhammad. (2012). "People Need Some Buddhism in Our Islam." Also see Mirza Tahir Ahmad. (1996). An Elementary Study of Islam.
10 Mirza Tahir Ahmad. (1996).
11 Royal Asiatic Society. (1830). Transactions of the Royal Asiatic Society of Great Britain and Ireland. Parbury, Allen, and Co. p. 311-312.

12 Godfrey Higgins. (1836). Anacalypsis, Vol. 2. p. 362.

13 S.N. Sadasivan. (2000). A Social History of India. P. 174.

14 S.N. Sadasivan. (2000). P. 174.

15 P.T. Srinivasa Iyengar. (1929). History of the Tamils – From the Earliest Times to 600 AD. P. 77.

16 Winthrop Sargeant. (1979). The Bhagavad Gita. P. 13-14.

17 S.N. Sadasivan. (2000). P. 174.

18 My father came from the lowest caste, so our family name, Das, literally came to mean "black-skinned slave" (it originally meant "Black enemy"). For more on this story, see When the World was Black.

19 Pranab Chatergee. (2010). A Story of Ambivalent Modernization in Bangladesh and West Bengal. P. 107-108.

20 Godfrey Higgins. (1833).

21 Gupta, Gyan Swarup (1999), India: From Indus Valley Civilisation to Mauryas, Concept Publishing Company

22 Rankin, Aidan. (2010). Many-Sided Wisdom: A New Politics of the Spirit. John Hunt Publishing.

23 W. Crooke. (1900).

24 John Calloway. (1829). Yakkun nattannawā. Oriental Translation Fund.

25 Overmyer, Daniel L. (1995) p. 126.

26 Keightley, David N. (1999). "The Shang." Cambridge History of Ancient China. Cambridge University Press. p. 253.

27 Keightley, David. (1999). p. 129.

28 Eberhard, Wolfram. (1969). A History of China. p. 23.

29 Keightley, David. (1999). p. 252.

30 Winters, Clyde-Ahmad. (1984). "Blacks in Ancient China, Pt. 1: The Founders of Xia and Shang." Journal of Black Studies. p. 8.

31 Lewis, Mark Edward. (1999). "Warring States Political History." Cambridge History of Ancient China. p. 637.

32 Ferrie, Helke. (Apr 1995). "A Conversation with K.C. Chang (in Reports)." Current Anthropology. Vol. 36, No. 2. p. 321. Chang also notes that marijuana is likely to have been one of the paraphernalia of the shaman of the Shang and Zhou periods, for which they were criticized by the Han. p. 320.

33 Quatrefages, Armand de. (1885). p. 159. Of pre-Aryan (that is, Black) India, the same has been said: "...Shamanism was a way of life of the original people before its Brahmaryan conquest." Jain, Ramchandra. (Ed.). Ancient India by Megasthenes and Arrian. p. xlvi.

34 Brunson, James E. (1985). Black Jade: African Presence in the Ancient East and Other Essays. p. 29.

35 Keightley, David. (1999). p. 240.

36 Li Chi. (1928) p. 245. These "black dwarfs" were said to have inhabited what is now Anhui province during the third century A.D. Carl Whiting Bishop. (1934). p. 300

37 Liu, James J.Y. (1967). The Chinese Knight Errant. Routledge.

38 Liu, James J.Y. (1967).

39 Granet, Marcel. (1930). Chinese Civilization. Trans. Kathleen E. Innes and Mabel R Brailsford. p. 9. Other accounts list Fu Xi, Sui Ren and Shen Nung. Chang, Kwang-Chih. (1999) p. 70.

40 Inman, Thomas. (1915). Ancient Pagan and Modern Christian Symbolism.

2nd ed. Quoted in Rogers, J.A. (1967) p. 266.

41 Granet, Marcel. (1930). p. 10.

42 The idea of divine and royal sibling/spouse relations is a feature common to the mythos associated with divinities and royal personages in Egypt, greater Africa, the Near East, and any number of locales anciently populated by Blacks. Blacks today are perhaps the only people still to refer to each other as "brother" and "sister" regardless of blood relation. Metaphoric terms of endearment should, obviously, not be taken to confirm incestuous relations, as has often been done, without the conclusive evidence (like the kind that does, on the other hand, exist for many of the early royal families of Europe).

43 Tai Ping Yu Lan (Taiping Anthologies for the Emperor). "Nu Wa Makes Men." Chinese Myths and Fantasies.
www.chinavista/experience/story/story2.html

44 Pei An Ping. "New Progress in Rice Agriculture and the Origin of Civilization." Hunan Archaeological Research Institute. trans. Feng, Simon and Elaine Wong. www.carleton.ca/~bgordon/Rice/papers/pei99.htm

45 Chang, Kwang-Chih. (1999). p. 71.

46 Roberts, J.A.G. (1996). p. 14.

47 Roberts, J.A.G. (1996). p. 19.

48 Bishop, Carl Whiting. (Sep 1934). "The Beginnings of North and South in China." Pacific Affairs, Vol. 7, Issue 3. p. 312-3.

49 This was not a creation ex nihilo or in vacuo, as Kwang-Chih Chang notes in the Cambridge History of Ancient China, p. 68. Rather, it was a making of something new from some other thing, or substance that already existed. Chang says this transformation "closed an earlier world and opened a modern one." The author of the book of Genesis uses a Hebrew word (beresheth) in beginning the Judaic Creation story, which means roughly the same thing. That is, God formed, or remade, the heavens and earth, depending on whose translation one subscribes to. We explain this in The Science of Self, Vol. 1.

50 Wu Zheng. Wu Yun Li Nianji. Quoted in Chang (1999) p. 67.

51 Chang, Kwang-Chih. (1999) p. 67.

52 Eberhard, Wolfram. (1965). Folktales of China. P. 199.

53 Eberhard, Wolfram. (1965). p. 3. The men "baked by the sun" is reminiscent of the representation of the zhong, with its three men under the sun.

54 Eberhard, Wolfram. (1969) p. 23.

55 Chang, Kwang-Chih. (1999) p. 66.

56 Yi Wen Lei Ju (Classified Anthology of Literary Works). Quoted in "Pangu Separates the Sky from the Earth." Chinese Myths and Fantasies.
www.chinavista/experience/story/story1.html

57 Radcliffe-Brown, A.R. (1948). The Andaman Islanders. p. 192

58 Shao, Paul. (1983). The Origin of Ancient American Cultures. p. 207.

59 Chang, Kwang-Chih. (1980). Shang Civilization. p. 210.

60 Chang, Kwang-Chih. (1980).

61 Shao, Paul. (1983) p. 207.

62 S.D. Gamble. (1954).Ting Hsien: A North China Rural Community. P. 420.

63 Micha F. Lindemans. (2004). "Cai-shen." Encyclopedia Mythica.
www.pantheon.org/articles/c/cai-shen.html

64 W. Crooke. (1900).

65 Czaja, Michael. (1974). Gods of Myth and Stone: Phallicism In Japanese Folk

Religion. Weatherhill.

66 Soka Gakkai International. (2012). "Daikoku." The Soka Gakkai Dictionary of Buddhism. www.sgilibrary.org

67 Michael Ashkenazi. (2003). Handbook of Japanese Mythology. P. 150.

68 Tokyo Daigaku. (1959). Journal: Anthropology, Volume 2. p. 144.

69 Cynthia Hallen. (1999). "The Ainu Language." http://linguistics.byu.edu/classes/ling450ch/reports/ainu.htm

70 A.A.J. Jansen, Susan Parkinson, A.F.S. Robertson. (1990). Food and Nutrition in Fiji: Food production, composition, and intake, Volume One. Institute of Pacific Studies. P. 4.

71 Ian Osborn. (2008). The Rough Guide to Fiji. Penguin.

72 Donald F. Lach, Edwin J. Van Kley. (1993). Asia in the Making of Europe, Volume III: A Century of Advance. Book 4: East Asia. University of Chicago Press. p. 1912-1913.

73 E.C.L. von Bunsen. (1867). The Keys of Saint Peter. Longmans and Green.

74 H.P. Blavatsky. (1894). Lucifer: A Theosophical Magazine, Vol. XIV. P. 502.

75 George Rawlinson. (1884). "The Religions of the Ancient World." Humboldt Library of Science, Issue 62. Humboldt Publishing Co. p. 31.

76 Supreme Understanding. (2013). When the World Was Black, Part Two. Supreme Design Publishing.

77 Wendy Donger. (Ed.). (1999). "Slavic Religion." Merriam-Webster's Encyclopedia of World Religions. P. 1016.

78 Gerald Massey. (1883). "Typology of the Mythical Male Twins." The Natural Genesis: Or, Second Part of A Book of the Beginnings, Volume 1. Williams and Norgate. p. 484-486.

79 W.E.B. Du Bois. (1915). The Negro.

80 Josiah Priest. (1852). Bible Defence of Slavery: And Origin, Fortunes, and History of the Negro Race. W.S. Brown. p. 70.

81 True Islam (Wesley Muhammad). (1999). The Book of God. All in All Publishing. p. 99-100.

82 John G. Jackson. (1939). Ethiopia and the Origin of Civilization.

83 Joel Augustus Rogers. (1944). Sex and Race: The Old World. P. 265.

84 Henry J. Fox. (1876). The Student's Common-place Book: A Cyclopedia of Illustration and Fact, Volume 1. p. 102.

85 Godfrey Higgins. (1833). Anacalypsis. Vol. I., p. 138.

86 Just search Wikipedia for "Black Christ" or "Black Madonna" and you'll find the lists and locations.

87 Godfrey Higgins. (1833). p. 138.

88 Wesley Muhammad. (Dec 24 2012). "Color struck: America's White Jesus is a global export and false product." The Final Call.

89 W. Crooke. (1900).

90 Maynard Shipley. Sex and The Garden of Eden Myth, Little Blue Book No.1188. p. 50–51.

91 This makes sense, as Heliopolis was an important scientific center in the ancient Nile Valley. See Supreme Understanding and C'BS Alife Allah. (2012). The Science of Self, Volume One. Supreme Design Publishing.

92 William Drummond. (1825). Origines: or, Remarks on the origin of several empires, states and cities. P. 320.

93 Diop, Cheikh Anta. (1974). The African Origin of Civilization: Myth or

Reality. Cited in Supreme Understanding and C'BS Alife Allah. (2012). The Science of Self, Volume One. Supreme Design Publishing.

94 Christopher Ehret. (1983). "Egyptian Religion." The New Encyclopedia Britannica. Vol. 6. p. 508.

95 Three Initiates. (2012). The Kybalion: The Seven Ancient Principles. Two Horizons Press.

96 Miriam Lichtheim. (Trans.). Ancient Egyptian Literature, Volume I: The Old and Middle Kingdom.

97 Gerald Massey. (1907). Ancient Egypt, The Light of The World, Vol. 1, p. 250.

98 Gerald Massey. (1907). p. 250.

99 W. Crooke. (1900).

100 Gerald Massey. (1907). p. 250.

101 Alaistar Sooke. (June 2013). "How Egyptian God Bes Gave the Christian Devil his Looks." BBC News. www.bbc.com/culture/story/20130619-how-the-devil-got-his-looks

102 Sidney Langford Hinde. (1901). The Last of the Masai. William Heinemann.

103 Sidney Langford Hinde. (1901). The Last of the Masai. William Heinemann.

104 Luke L. Plunkett. (1915). "Religious Beliefs of Equatorial Africans." The American Catholic Quarterly Review, Volume 40.

105 Harry Hamilton Johnston. (1904). The Uganda Protectorate. p. 831.

106 Luke L. Plunkett. (1915).

107 Luke L. Plunkett. (1915).

108 John S. Mbiti. (1970). Concepts of God in Africa. Praeger Publishers, p. 91.

109 John S. Mbiti. (1970). p. 12.

110 Nathaniel Samuel Murrell. (Ed.). (1998). Chanting Down Babylon: A Rastafari Reader. P. 137.

111 John S. Mbiti. (1970). p. 16.

112 John S. Mbiti. (1970). p. 25.

113 John S. Mbiti. (1970). p. 29.

114 John S. Mbiti. (1970). p. 94.

115 Robert P. Scharlemann. (Ed.) (1985). Naming God. Paragon House. p. 69.

116 Regents of the University of Michigan. "Olokun." Mythology. Last accessed Feb 4th 1999. http://www.windows.umich.edu/cgi-bin/tour.cgi?link=/mythology/olokun_sea.html

117 Robert P. Scharlemann. (1985). p. 71.

118 John S. Mbiti. (1970). p. 96.

119 John S. Mbiti. (1970). p. 150.

120 John S. Mbiti. (1970). p. 171-172.

121 John S. Mbiti. (1970). p. 172.

122 John S. Mbiti. (1970). p. 92.

123 John S. Mbiti. (1970). p. 171.

124 John S. Mbiti. (1970). p. 114.

125 Harry Sawyerr. (1970). God: Ancestor or Creator? Longman Group. p. 40.

126 Harry Sawyerr. (1970). p. 50.

127 Owens, D.W., ed. (1999).

128 J.B. Danquah. (1944). The Akan Doctrine of God.

129 S. Johnson. (1921). A History of the Yorubas. P. 3.

130 S. Johnson. (1921). P. 143.

131 Harry Sawyerr. (1970). p. 14-15.

132 Harry Sawyerr. (1970). p. 8.
133 Regents of the University of Michigan. "Shango." Mythology. Last accessed Feb 4th 1999. www.windows.umich.edu/cgi-bin/tour.cgi?link=/mythology/shango_storm.html.
134 Harry Sawyerr. (1970). p. 55.
135 Rev. P. Hadfield. (1949). Traits of Divine Kingship in Africa. London Watts & Co. p. 10-15.
136 Rev. P. Hadfield. (1949). p. 11-15.
137 Rev. P. Hadfield. (1949). p. 11-15.
138 Mohammed Hassen. (1994).The Oromo of Ethiopia. p. 137.
139 Rev. P. Hadfield. (1949). p. 11.
140 A. Hampâté Bâ. (Aug-Sep 1979). "Tongues that span the centuries: The faithful guardians of Africa's oral tradition." The UNESCO Courier. UNESCO.
141 P. Bohannan, P.D. Curtin. (1995). Africa and Africans, Waveland Press. p. 68
142 John S. Mbiti. (1970). p. 70.
143 Placide Tempels. (1959). Bantu Philosophy. Presence Africaine.
144 John S. Mbiti. (1970). p. 53.
145 J.B. Danquah. (1944).
146 J.B. Danquah. (1944). P. 169.
147 Abisha S. Hudson. (1889). p. 30.
148 W.E.B. Du Bois. (1946). The World and Africa. The Viking Press.
149 Josiah Priest, (1853). Bible Defence of Slavery, Or, The Origin, History, and Fortunes of the Negro Race. W.S. Brown. p. 71.
150 Josiah Priest, (1853). p. 71.
151 John G. Jackson. (1939). Ethiopia and the Origin of Civilization.
152 David MacRitchie. (1893). Fians, Fairies, and Picts. Citing the example of the Yesso dwarfs of Japan, MacRitchie adds the following explanation: "In that instance, we see before our eyes the whole process by which a real race has been transformed into an unreal impossibility, within a period of two centuries or so. Had the extinction (or modification by intermarriage or by the processes of evolution) of those Yesso dwarfs taken place a thousand years earlier, the difficulty of identifying them would have been greatly increased."
153 David MacRitchie. (1884). Ancient and Modern Britons: A Retrospect. P. 58.
154 David MacRitchie. (1884). P. 440.
155 David MacRitchie. (1884). P. 440.
156 Helene Guerber. (1895). Myths of Northern Lands. P. 217-218.
157 Robert Grant Haliburton. (1897). How a race of pygmies was found in North Africa and Spain.
158 Gerald Massey. (1907). p. 373-374.
159 A.E. Waite and Pamela Colman Smith. (1911). The Pictorial Key to the Tarot.
160 Barber, Malcolm (1994). The New Knighthood: A History of the Order of the Temple.
161 Knight, Richard Payne. (1865). A Discourse on the Worship of Priapus. P. 198.
162 John G. Jackson. (1939). Ethiopia and the Origin of Civilization.
163 Harold G. Lawrence, (Jun-Jul 1962). "African Explorers of the New World," The Crisis, p. 322.
164 Paul Schellhas. (1910). Representation of deities of the Maya manuscripts, Volume 4, Issues 1-3. Salem Press. p. 35.
165 Paul Schellhas. (1910).

166 Peterson, Frederick. (1959). Ancient Mexico. G.P. Putnam's Sons, p. 50.

167 Supreme Understanding. (2013). When the World Was Black, Part Two. Supreme Design Publishing.

168 Supreme Understanding. (2013).

169 Guilhem Olivier. (2003). Mockeries and Metamorphoses of an Aztec God: Tezcatlipoca, "Lord of the Smoking Mirror". translated by Michel Besson.

170 Guilhem Olivier. (2003).

171 Lewis Spence. (2010). Myths of Mexico and Peru. P. 114.

172 Paul Schellhas. (1910).

173 Lewis Spence. (2010).P. 95.

174 Nicholas Bakalar. (Mar 2 2006). "Corn, Arrowroot Fossils in Peru Change Views on Pre-Inca Culture." National Geographic News. http://news.nationalgeographic.com/ news/2006/03/0302_060302_peru_corn.html

175 Clark Wissler, D. C. Duvall. (1908). Mythology of the Blackfoot Indians, Volume 2, Parts 1-3. The Trustees.

176 Clark Wissler, D. C. Duvall. (1908).

177 Clark Wissler, D. C. Duvall. (1908).

178 Clark Wissler, D. C. Duvall. (1908).

179 Clark Wissler, D. C. Duvall. (1908).

180 Smithsonian Institution, Bureau of American Ethnology. (1912). Handbook of American Indians North of Mexico: N-Z. U.S. Government Printing Office.

181 John Swanton. (1905). Haida Texts and Myths. Smithsonian Institution, Bureau of American Ethnology, Government Printing Office.

182 Smithsonian Institution, Bureau of American Ethnology. (1912). Handbook of American Indians North of Mexico: N-Z. U.S. Government Printing Office.

183 Luz Evelia Martín Del Campo-Hermosillo. (2010). Genderscape: The Ecology Of A Gendering Landscape. Unpublished dissertation. University of Florida. http://etd.fcla.edu/UF/UFE0041553/martindelcampo_l.pdf

184 Frank Gouldsmith Speck. (1909). Ethnology of the Yuchi Indians, Volume 1, Issue 1. University Museum. p. 107.

185 Frank Gouldsmith Speck. (1909). p. 107.

186 See Supreme Understanding. (2013). When the World was Black, Part One.

187 Ekkehart Malotki. (2000). Kokopelli: The Making of an Icon. Univ of Nebraska Press.

188 Leo Wiener. (1921). Africa and the Discovery of America, Vol. 3. p. 258.

189 Seymore H. Koenig. (2005). Acculturation in the Navajo Eden: New Mexico, 1550-1750. YBK Publishers.

190 D.S. McDonald (1998). "Intimacy and Empire: Indian-African Interaction in Spanish Colonial New Mexico, 1500-1800." American Indian Quarterly 22(1/2): 134-156.

191 C.A. Roberts; S. Roberts. (2006). New Mexico. p. 24–26.

192 Wilcomb E. Washburn. (1996). The Cambridge history of the native peoples of the Americas, Part 1. Cambridge University Press. p. 371.

193 Washington Matthews. (1901)."The Treatment of Ailing Gods." Originally read at the Twelfth Annual Meeting of the American Folk-Lore Society, Baltimore, Md., December 28, 1900. The Journal of American Folklore, Volume 14. p. 20-23.

194 Edward S. Curtis. (1907). The North American Indian. Vol. 1.

195 Harold Fuchs. (2005). "Black Hactcin." Encyclopedia Mythica.
www.pantheon.org/articles/b/black_hactcin.html
196 David Adams Leeming. (2010).Creation Myths of the World, Vol. 1. P. 42.
197 Harold Fuchs. (2005).
198 Richard Willows. (2012). "Black Hactcin and the Myth untold."
http://prezi.com/yqh2twwj9gt_/black-hactcin-and-the-myth-untold/
199 Bancroft, Hubert H. (1883). The Native Races of the Pacific States. Vol. 3.
200 Goetz, Delia and Sylvanus G. Goetz. (1950). The Popol Vuh. Trans. Adrian
Recinos. University of Oklahoma Press.
201 Goetz, Delia and Sylvanus G. Goetz. (1950).
202 Ermilo Abreu Gomez, (1992). The Popol Vuh. Dante. p. 9-10.
203 Runoko Rashidi. "The African Roots of Humanity and Civilization."
204 George Kibbe Turner. (1920). Hagar's Hoard. Aflred A. Knopf.
205 Benjamin Sevitch. "When Black Gods Preached on Earth" Journal of
Communication and Religion.
206 Stephen Graham. (1920). Children of the Slaves. Macmillan. p. 182-185.
207 Stephen Graham. (1920). p. 182-185.
208 Stephen Graham. (1920). p. 182-185.
209 Supreme Understanding and C'BS Alife Allah. (2012). The Science of Self,
Volume One. Supreme Design Publishing.
210 American Missionary Association. (1928). The American Missionary, Vol.
82. p. 60.
211 Supreme Understanding and C'BS Alife Allah. (2012). The Science of Self,
Volume One. Supreme Design Publishing.
212 Shabazz Adew Allah. "The Mystery of the Seventh Seal." Five Percent
Concepts. It was Allah, Adew says, who took the secret of God out of the
temple and into the streets, just as the Old Testament ends with God in the
temple with Elijah, and the New Testament begins with God teaching in person
in the streets. Some point out that Matthew (whose named is attached to the
first Gospel) was also the name of Allah's first student.

ALSO FROM OUR COMPANY

How to Hustle and Win, Part 1: A Survival Guide for the Ghetto

By Supreme Understanding
Foreword by the Real Rick Ross

This is the book that started it all. Now an international bestseller, this book has revolutionized the way people think of "urban literature." It offers a street-based analysis of social problems, plus practical solutions that anyone can put to use.

CLASS	PAGES	RETAIL	RELEASE
I-1	336	$19.95	Jun. 2008

ISBN: 978-0-9816170-0-8

How to Hustle and Win, Part 2: Rap, Race, and Revolution

By Supreme Understanding
Foreword by Stic.man of Dead Prez

Seen here in its original green cover, the controversial follow-up to *How to Hustle and Win* digs even deeper into the problems we face, and how we can solve them. Part One focused on personal change, and Part Two explores the bigger picture of changing the entire hood.

CLASS	PAGES	RETAIL	RELEASE
I-1	384	$19.95	Apr. 2009

ISBN: 978-0-9816170-9-1

Knowledge of Self: A Collection of Wisdom on the Science of Everything in Life

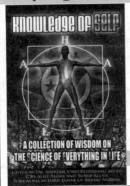

Edited by Supreme Understanding, C'BS Alife Allah, and Sunez Allah, Foreword by Lord Jamar of Brand Nubian

Who are the Five Percent? Why are they here? In this book, over 50 Five Percenters from around the world speak for themselves, providing a comprehensive introduction to the esoteric teachings of the Nation of Gods and Earths.

CLASS	PAGES	RETAIL	RELEASE
I-2	256	$19.95	Jul. 2009

ISBN: 978-0-9816170-2-2

The Hood Health Handbook, Volume One (Physical Health)

Edited by Supreme Understanding and C'BS Alife Allah, Foreword by Dick Gregory

Want to know why Black and brown people are so sick? This book covers the many "unnatural causes" behind our poor health, and offers hundreds of affordable and easy-to-implement solutions.

CLASS	PAGES	RETAIL	RELEASE
PH-1	480	$19.95	Nov. 2010

ISBN: 978-1-935721-32-1

The Hood Health Handbook, Volume Two (Mental Health)

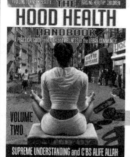

Edited by Supreme Understanding and C'BS Alife Allah

This volume covers mental health, how to keep a healthy home, raising healthy children, environmental issues, and dozens of other issues, all from the same down-to-earth perspective as Volume One.

CLASS	PAGES	RETAIL	RELEASE
MH-1	480	$19.95	Nov. 2010

ISBN: 978-1-935721-33-8

A Taste of Life: 1,000 Vegetarian Recipes from Around the World

Edited by Supreme Understanding and Patra Afrika

This cookbook makes it easy to become vegetarian. In addition to over 1,000 recipes from everywhere you can think of, plus over 100 drink and smoothie recipes, this book also teaches how to transition your diet, what to shop for, how to cook, as well as a guide to nutrients and vitamins.

CLASS	PAGES	RETAIL	RELEASE
W-1	400	$19.95	Jun. 2011

ISBN: 978-1-935721-10-9

La Brega: Como Sobrevivir En El Barrio

By Supreme Understanding

Thanks to strong demand coming from Spanish-speaking countries, we translated our groundbreaking How to Hustle and Win into Spanish, and added new content specific to Latin America. Because this book's language is easy to follow, it can also be used to brush up on your Spanish.

CLASS	PAGES	RETAIL	RELEASE
0-1	336	$14.95	Jul. 2009

ISBN: 978-0981617-08-4

Locked Up but Not Locked Down: A Guide to Surviving the American Prison System

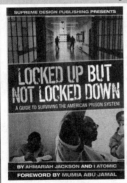

By Ahmariah Jackson and IAtomic Allah
Foreword by Mumia Abu Jamal

This book covers what it's like on the inside, how to make the most of your time, what to do once you're out, and how to stay out. Features contributions from over 50 insiders, covering city jails, state and federal prisons, women's prisons, juvenile detention, and international prisons.

CLASS	PAGES	RETAIL	RELEASE
J-1	288	$24.95	Jul. 2012

ISBN: 978-1935721-00-0

The Science of Self: Man, God, and the Mathematical Language of Nature

By Supreme Understanding and C'BS Alife Allah

How did the universe begin? Is there a pattern to everything that happens? What's the meaning of life? What does science tell us about the depths of our SELF? Who and what is God? This may be one of the deepest books you can read.

CLASS	PAGES	RETAIL	RELEASE
I-4	360	$29.95	Jun. 2012

ISBN: 978-1935721-67-3

When the World was Black, Part One: Prehistoric Cultures

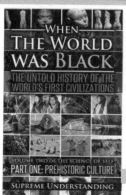

By Supreme Understanding
Foreword by Runoko Rashid

When does Black history begin? Certainly not with slavery. In two volumes, historian Supreme Understanding explores over 200,000 years of Black history from every corner of the globe. Part One covers the first Black communities to settle the world, establishing its first cultures and traditions. Their stories are remarkable.

CLASS	PAGES	RETAIL	RELEASE
I-3	400	$24.95	Feb. 2013

ISBN: 978-1-935721-04-8

When the World Was Black, Part Two: Ancient Civilizations

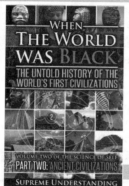

By Supreme Understanding

Part Two covers the ancient Black civilizations that gave birth to the modern world. Black people built the first urban civilizations in Africa, Asia, Europe, and the Americas. And every claim in these books is thoroughly documented with reputable sources. Do you want to know the story of your ancestors? You should. We study the past to see what the future will bring.

CLASS	PAGES	RETAIL	RELEASE
I-3	400	$24.95	Feb. 2013

ISBN: 978-1-935721-05-5

When the World was Black, Parts One and Two (Hardcover)

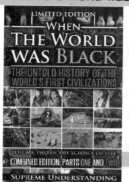

By Supreme Understanding

An incredible limited edition that combines Part One and Part Two into a single book, cased in an embossed clothbound hardcover and dust jacket. Autographed and numbered, this collector's item also includes both sets of full-color inserts.

CLASS	PAGES	RETAIL	RELEASE
I-3	800	$74.95	Dec. 2013

Only available direct from publisher.

Black Rebellion: Eyewitness Accounts of Major Slave Revolts

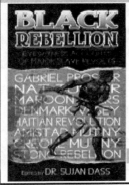

Edited by Dr. Sujan Dass

Who will tell the stories of those who refused to be slaves? What about those who fought so effectively that they forced their slavers to give up? Black Rebellion is a collection of historical "eyewitness" accounts of dozens of major revolts and uprisings, from the U.S. to the Caribbean, as well as a history of slavery and revolt.

CLASS	PAGES	RETAIL	RELEASE
P-3	272	$19.95	May 2010

ISBN: 978-0-981617-04-6

The Heroic Slave

By Frederick Douglass

Most people don't know that Douglass wrote a novel...or that, in this short novel, he promoted the idea of violent revolt. By this time in his life, the renowned abolitionist was seeing things differently. This important piece of history comes with *David Walker's Appeal*, all in one book.

CLASS	PAGES	RETAIL	RELEASE
P-3	160	$19.95	Apr. 2011

ISBN: 978-1-935721-27-7

David Walker's Appeal

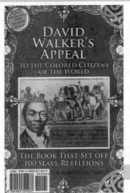

By David Walker

This is one of the most important, and radical, works ever published against slavery. Rather than call for an end by peaceful means, Walker called for outright revolution. His calls may have led to over 100 revolts, including those described in *Black Rebellion*. This important piece of history comes with Douglass' *The Heroic Slave*, which it may have helped inspire.

CLASS	PAGES	RETAIL	RELEASE
P-3	160	$19.95	Apr. 2011

ISBN: 978-1-935721-27-7

Darkwater: Voices from Within the Veil, Annotated Edition

By W.E.B. Du Bois

This book makes Du Bois' previous work, like *Souls of Black Folk*, seem tame by comparison. *Darkwater* is revolutionary, uncompromising, and unconventional in both its content and style, addressing the plight of Black women, the rise of a Black Messiah, a critical analysis of white folks, and the need for outright revolution.

CLASS	PAGES	RETAIL	RELEASE
I-4	240	$19.95	Jun. 2011

ISBN: 978-0-981617-07-7

The African Abroad: The Black Man's Evolution in Western Civilization, Volume One

By William Henry Ferris

Who would think a book written in 1911 could cover so much? Ferris, chairman of the UNIA, speaks up for the Black man's role in Western civilization. He discusses a wealth of history, as well as some revolutionary Black theology, exploring the idea of man as God and God as man.

CLASS	PAGES	RETAIL	RELEASE
I-5	570	$29.95	Oct. 2012

ISBN: 978-1935721-66-6

The African Abroad: Volume Two

By William Henry Ferris

The second volume of Ferris' epic covers important Black biographies of great leaders, ancient and modern. He tells the stories of forty "Black Immortals." He also identifies the African origins of many of the world's civilizations, including ancient Egypt, Akkad, Sumer, India, and Europe.

CLASS	PAGES	RETAIL	RELEASE
I-5	330	$19.95	Oct. 2012

ISBN: 978-1-935721-69-7

From Poverty to Power: The Realization of Prosperity and Peace

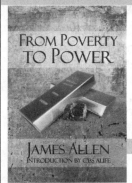

By James Allen

Want to transform your life? James Allen, the author of the classic *As a Man Thinketh,* explores how we can turn struggle and adversity into power and prosperity. This inspirational text teaches readers about their innate strength and the immense power of the conscious mind.

CLASS	PAGES	RETAIL	RELEASE
I-3	144	$19.95	May 2010

ISBN: 978-0-981617-05-3

Daily Meditations: A Year of Guidance on the Meaning of Life

By James Allen

Need a guidebook to a productive and healthy year? This is it. James Allen delivers another great work in this book, this time offering 365 days of inspiration and guidance on life's greatest challenges. This book includes sections for daily notes.

CLASS	PAGES	RETAIL	RELEASE
C-3	208	$19.95	Apr. 2013

ISBN: 978-1-935721-08-6

The Kybalion: The Seven Ancient Egyptian Laws _

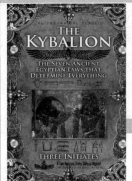

By the Three Initiates

Thousands of years ago, the ancients figured out a set of principles that govern the universe. In *The Kybalion*, these laws are explored and explained. This edition includes research into the authorship of the book, and where the laws came from.

CLASS	PAGES	RETAIL	RELEASE
C-4	130	$19.95	Oct. 2012

ISBN: 978-1-935721-25-3

Real Life is No Fairy Tale (w/ Companion CD)

By Sujan Dass and Lord Williams

Looking for a children's book that teaches about struggle? Written for school age children, this full-color hardcover book is composed entirely in rhyme, and the images are as real as they get. Includes a CD with an audio book, animated video, review questions, and printable worksheets and activities.

CLASS	PGS	RETAIL	RELEASE
CD-4	36+	$16.95	Jun. 2010

ISBN: 978-0-9816170-2-2

Aesop's Fables: 101 Classic Tales and Timeless Lessons

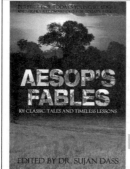

Edited by Dr. Sujan Dass

What's better to teach our children than life lessons? This easy-to-read collection of classic tales told by an African storyteller uses animals to teach valuable moral lessons. This edition includes dozens of black-and-white images to accompany the timeless fables. Color them in!

CLASS	PAGES	RETAIL	RELEASE
CD-3	112	$14.95	Feb. 2013

ISBN: 978-1-935721-07-9

Heritage Playing Cards (w/ Companion Booklet)

Designed by Sujan Dass

No more European royalty! This beautiful deck of playing cards features 54 full-color characters from around the world and a 16-page educational booklet on international card games and the ethnic backgrounds of the people on the cards.

CLASS	PGS	RETAIL	RELEASE
CD-2	16+	$14.95	May 2010

UPC: 05105-38587

Black God: An Introduction to the World's Religions and their Black Gods

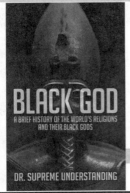

By Supreme Understanding

Have you ever heard that Christ was Black? What about the Buddha? They weren't alone. This book explores the many Black gods of the ancient world, from Africa to Europe, Asia, and Australia, all the way to the Americas. Who were they? Why were they worshipped? And what does this mean for us today?

CLASS	PAGES	RETAIL	RELEASE
C-3	200	$19.95	Jan. 2014

ISBN: 978-1-935721-12-3

Black People Invented Everything

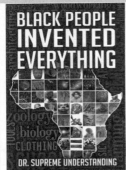

By Supreme Understanding

In *The Science of Self* we began exploring the origins of everything that modern civilization depends on today. In this book, we get into specifics, showing how Black people invented everything from agriculture to zoology, with dozens of pictures and references to prove it!

CLASS	PAGES	RETAIL	RELEASE
I-3	256	$29.95	Feb. 2020

ISBN: 978-1-935721-13-0

The Yogi Science of Breath: A Complete Manual of the Ancient Philosophy of the East

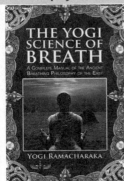

By Yogi Ramacharaka

A classic text on the science of breathing, one of the most ignored, yet important, aspects of our physical and emotional health. This book has been used by both martial arts experts and legendary jazz musicians. This edition explores the "secret science" of breath, and where its mysterious author learned such teachings.

CLASS	PAGES	RETAIL	RELEASE
PH-4	112	$14.95	Apr. 2012

ISBN: 978-1-935721-34-5

How to Get Our Books

To better serve our readers, we've streamlined the way we handle book orders. Here are some of the ways you can find our books.

In Stores

You can find our books in just about any Black bookstore or independent bookseller. If you don't find our titles on the shelves, just request them by name and publisher. Most bookstores can order our titles directly from us (via our site) or from the distributors listed below. We also provide a listing of retailers who carry our books at www.bestblackbooks.com

Online (Wholesale)

Now, you can visit our sites (like www.supremeunderstanding.com or www.bestblackbooks.com) to order wholesale quantities direct from us, the publisher. From our site, we ship heavily discounted case quantities to distributors, wholesalers, retailers, and local independent resellers (like yourself – just try it!). The discounts are so deep, you can afford to GIVE books away if you're not into making money.

Online (Retail)

If you're interested in single "retail" copies, you can now find them online at Amazon.com, or you can order them via mail order by contacting one of the mail order distributors listed below. You can also find many of our titles as eBooks in the Amazon Kindle, Nook, or Apple iBooks systems. You may also find full-length videobook or audiobook files available, but nothing beats the pass-around potential of a real book!

By Mail Order

Please contact any of the following Black-owned distributors to order our books! For others, visit our site.

Afrikan World Books
2217 Pennsylvania Ave.
Baltimore, MD 21217
(410) 383-2006

Lushena Books
607 Country Club Dr
Bensenville, IL 60106
(800) 785-1545

Special Needs X-Press
927 Old Nepperhan Ave
Yonkers, NY 10703
(914) 623-7007